HEART
— OF THE —
MATTER

HEART
— OF THE —
MATTER

WHAT 100 YEARS OF LIVING
HAVE TAUGHT ME

RUSSELL M.
NELSON

DESERET
BOOK

SALT LAKE CITY, UTAH

Visit us at deseretbook.com

Library of Congress Cataloging-in-Publication Data

(CIP data on file)
ISBN 978-1-63993-256-6

Printed in the United States of America
Lake Book Manufacturing, LLC, Melrose Park, IL

10 9 8 7 6 5 4 3 2 1

CONTENTS

INTRODUCTION

Now that I am in my hundredth year, I have the rare opportunity of reflecting on a century of living.

I was born during the Roaring Twenties, when the world was still emerging from the devastating effects of World War I. I have lived to see far too many other wars, the Great Depression, the rise of terrorism, and even a worldwide pandemic.

Thankfully, I have also witnessed remarkable strides forward for humanity. I marvel at the countless innovations that have transformed the world around me. I remember witnessing the first television broadcasts that were little more than a grainy picture in black and white and then the awe of antibiotics such as penicillin that revolutionized medicine. I have seen everything from the advent of jet engines, radar, and nuclear power to the transformational nature of the transistor and integrated circuits that laid the foundation for the digital age.

In recent years, I have experienced the explosive growth of the Internet and the rise of social media platforms that have fundamentally changed how people communicate and share information. I have seen the world become more interconnected and globalized while also grappling with the challenges these advancements bring. During my life I've seen the automobile industry go from producing Ford's Model T Touring Car to electric vehicles of almost every brand. And now we are becoming acquainted with artificial intelligence and the dramatic leap this innovation represents. These advances are fascinating.

I have witnessed numerous political breakthroughs in my lifetime. I well remember the end of World War II in 1945 and the establishment of the United Nations. I was stirred as the Civil Rights Movement in the 1950s and 1960s brought about much-needed progress toward racial equality in the United States. I traveled frequently throughout Eastern Europe in the 1980s and, like the rest of the world, celebrated the fall of the Berlin Wall in 1989 and the major advancements throughout Eastern Europe that followed. I have seen the rise and fall of apartheid in South Africa and the subsequent election of Nelson Mandela as that country's first Black president.

These breakthroughs, along with countless others, have shown me that even in the midst of adversity and conflict, humanity has the capacity for growth, understanding, compassion, and progress.

The year I was born, The Church of Jesus Christ of Latter-day Saints had a membership just shy of 598,000. There were six operating temples, 90 stakes, 25 missions, and 867 missionaries. President Heber J. Grant was President of the Church. Elder David O. McKay was superintendent of the Sunday School and Elder George Albert Smith was superintendent of the Young Men's Mutual Improvement Association, both serving in those capacities as Apostles. Clarissa Smith Williams was General President of the Relief Society, Martha

Horne Tingey was General President of the Young Women Mutual Improvement Association, and Louie Bouton Felt was General President of the Primary.

The October 1924 general conference, held just three weeks after I was born, was the first to be broadcast by radio. President Heber J. Grant opened the conference proceedings with the following remarks: "The exercises of today and throughout the conference are to be broadcasted; and it is estimated that in the neighborhood of a million people will be able to hear all that is said, provided they are listening in during the conference sessions. The radio is one of the most marvelous inventions man knows anything about. To have the voice carried for thousands of miles seems almost beyond comprehension."

General conference is now broadcast to tens of millions of people around the globe. It goes without saying that the Lord's Church, along with transmission of general conference to the world, has changed dramatically during my lifetime.

I have traveled the earth for many decades now to fulfill various Church leadership responsibilities, visiting at least 135 countries—some of them many times. Through these visits, I have witnessed many of the world's most dramatic changes firsthand. I have a deep love and respect for the peoples and cultures of the earth who have taught me so much and made my life so much richer.

Frequent travel and assignments internationally propelled me to study languages—seventeen, including English. (I'm still working on English.) For example, years ago when I was serving as General President of the Sunday School, I received an assignment to what was then East Germany. I had never studied German and did not understand anything I heard or read. I remember wondering why so many streets were labeled *Ein Bahn Strasse*, which, I eventually found out, meant "one-way street." I said to my wife, "I don't want to be stupid. I want to understand what I am reading and hearing. If I ever get another assignment to Germany, I am going to be tutored first." I did, and I was.

Years later, as a General Authority, I was assigned to participate in the Frankfurt Germany Temple dedication and, in one session, I was to lead the Hosanna Shout in Dutch. I went to the First Presidency's office and asked Brother F. Michael Watson, secretary to the First Presidency, if there had been a mistake in giving that assignment to me. He quickly replied, "Do you want me to ask the First Presidency if they made a mistake?" I understood his message and proceeded to be tutored in the Dutch language to fulfill the assignment. Learning new languages has increased my love for God, for Jesus Christ and His gospel, and for the peoples of various nations.

As I indulge in reflections about my centennial journey, I am grateful to have witnessed a century of unprecedented innovation, and I am optimistic about what the future holds for humanity.

My one-hundredth year of living gives me the chance to reflect on the most pivotal moments of my life. Let me single out three by calling attention to three symbols that represent those important eras or turning points: a library card, the artificial heart-lung machine, and a call to devote my life fully to serving the Lord.

The Library Card

First, the library card. I have always been curious. I have always wanted to understand how things work. As a boy, I obtained my own library card and convinced my mother to let me hop on the streetcar in Salt Lake City and ride it downtown to the library. I wasn't more than eight or nine years old when I did this on a regular basis.

Once at the library, I would spend hours pulling books from the stacks and devouring them. I read books on the nervous system, baseball, astronomy, American history, mammals—you name it. I was even intrigued by the Dewey Decimal System used to catalog books, and I memorized it. I'm not sure how many other youth at the time knew the Dewey Decimal System, but I did.

In my teens, I continued going to the library and also spent hours in little glass booths in local music stores listening to classical music. My heart was stirred by "Una Furtiva Lagrima," *The Pearl Fishers*, and so many others. This was the 1930s, and the Glenn Miller Orchestra, Benny Goodman, Louis Armstrong, and Tommy Dorsey were all the rage. I liked them too, but classical music spoke to my heart, which had been tutored by the sounds of my mother's exquisite soprano voice.

My library card was perhaps my first possession that opened new worlds to me. I loved learning and loved my parents for encouraging me to read and explore the world around me. From those earliest days, they encouraged my voracious thirst for information and knowledge, which continues to this day.

The Heart-Lung Machine

Second, the heart-lung machine.

At age seventeen, I entered the University of Utah. World War II was raging, and every branch of the military needed doctors. That urgency pushed me toward medicine. The war disrupted our lives in countless ways, including changing the school's calendar, which allowed me to work simultaneously on my bachelor's and MD degrees. I received my BA in 1945 and my MD in 1947, at age twenty-two.

I was fortunate to do my internship and postgraduate work at the University of Minnesota, then regarded as one of the most prestigious universities for surgical training. There I was mentored and tutored by critically acclaimed physiologists, surgeons, researchers, and innovators.

Before going to Minnesota for postgraduate work, I had never considered heart surgery as a profession—because there was no such thing at the time! In fact, in medical school I was taught that I must never touch the human heart or it would stop beating. One of my medical school textbooks, by Theodor Billroth, published in 1913, threatened that "a surgeon who would attempt such an operation should lose the respect of his colleagues."

The theory was that God had made the body in such a way that the heart was protected with a sternum, so "hands off!"

But then, through a serendipitous sequence of events, something happened that changed the direction of my career and my life. I landed a spot on a research team, led by Dr. Clarence Dennis. This team was striving to build one of the world's first artificial heart-lung machines. For everyone on that team, this was a giant leap into the unknown. We were developing a machine that would essentially take over a patient's circulation to allow surgery on a heart that was not beating—even though we still wondered if it were even possible to touch the human heart without permanently damaging it.

There were, of course, many starts, stops, laboratory messes, and false assumptions as we ventured into an entirely new area of medicine. We had no idea about optimum oxygen consumption rates or minimum flow rates or the influence of temperature on the rate of metabolism. It took us a year just to learn how to have blood flow outside of the body without clotting and then make it coagulate again so healing could take place in the surgical incision.

Gratefully, our many early failures were punctuated with periodic successes. Finally, in March 1951, Dr. Dennis and others performed the first open-heart operation on a human being using the machine our team had built. However, it was not my good fortune to be in the operating room that day.

In the middle of my surgical training, the Korean War began, and because I was highly susceptible to the draft, I enlisted in the army and became a first lieutenant in the army medical corps. I was initially assigned to the Walter Reed National Military Medical Center in Washington, D.C. Later I spent time in M.A.S.H. units on the Korean Peninsula. Both of those assignments were highly instructive—and in very different ways.

After fulfilling my military obligation, I spent a year on the Harvard service at Massachusetts General Hospital in Boston. During that period of surgical training, I felt like a boy on Christmas morning who had just received his first red wagon. The mental stimulation in Boston was fantastic! Surgeons at Mass. General performed operations like an artist paints a portrait. My time there was a prized opportunity to increase my knowledge and exponentially improve my skills as a surgeon. Ultimately, I returned to Minnesota to finish my residency and receive my Ph.D. degree.

I then returned to Utah, where I performed the first open-heart operation west of the Mississippi. That was November of 1955. I was the third surgeon in the United States to perform such an operation successfully. I then continued to teach and practice thoracic and cardiovascular surgery for roughly thirty years. I will say more about lessons learned during those years of surgical discovery throughout this book. Without question, however, my ventures with the heart-lung machine during its earliest stages of development changed the course of my professional life.

A Call to Serve

Third, a call to the ministry.

At age fifty-nine, and without warning, my life changed in a way

I never expected. I was called to serve as a member of the Quorum of the Twelve Apostles in The Church of Jesus Christ of Latter-day Saints. As had every Apostle before me, I left my professional career behind and turned my attention to teaching the gospel of Jesus Christ and ministering around the world to others in need. My career had been all about healing diseased hearts. But suddenly I realized that my life would now be devoted to a different—and even more profound—kind of healing of hearts. For forty years now, it has been my focus and joy to teach the restored gospel of Jesus Christ, which is a gospel of healing wounded hearts—hearts that are filled with grief, confusion, anxiety, or discouragement.

Thus, both my professional and apostolic roles have centered around the heart. Practicing medicine taught me that with even the finest skills a physician or surgeon can acquire, we as mortals have no healing power in and of ourselves. We did not create the body. God did. We must depend upon law—divine law—to know how to tend to the body medically in such a way that the body will heal itself.

I remember how thrilled we were to learn through those early experiments so many decades ago that the heart did not mind being touched. It would keep beating—if we did not violate the laws that govern how it functions. It was the study of medicine that taught me about law—divine law in particular, and the fact that divine law is irrefutable.

A healthy, functioning heart is central to the health and well-being of each of us. However, what I have learned as a servant and witness of Jesus Christ is that a healthy physical heart is only half of our challenge. I take seriously the injunction to love God with all of our hearts, because loving Him is what keeps us vibrant.

The heart is the organ that keeps us alive physically, and it is also the organ that symbolically propels us forward emotionally and spiritually and gives the greatest meaning to our lives. From my point of view, the heart is at the very heart of everything meaningful in life.

I cannot speak of things of the heart without mentioning my family. My wife Dantzel and I were blessed with a large family—nine daughters and one son. We have fifty-seven grandchildren, 160 great-grandchildren, and one great-great-grandson—and counting. In 2005 Dantzel passed away suddenly and our family was devastated. She was the heart of our home and family.

Later, I was blessed to marry again, to Wendy Watson, a university professor. She has filled my life with joy and enriched our family in very distinctive ways. I cannot imagine life without her. My treasured family relationships have made life so fulfilling. My family members truly have my heart!

How I Hope This Book Benefits You

In January 2018, at age ninety-three, I was called by the Lord to serve as President of The Church of Jesus Christ of Latter-day Saints. This privilege and responsibility has underscored one of the profound learnings that 100 years of living have taught me—that divine laws and truths govern our lives, whether we realize it or not.

The laws or truths I will share in this book are not merely ideas I have studied and examined; they are the very essence of my life's experiences. I have come to depend on these essential laws and principles to improve each day as a man and as a husband; nurture meaningful connections with my children, grandchildren, and great-grandchildren; become a heart surgeon; build bridges of understanding with people the world over; teach the restored gospel of Jesus Christ throughout the world; lead a religion whose members are found in more than two hundred countries and whose head is

Jesus Christ; and serve the Lord, His people, and the world in more ways than I ever thought possible.

It is these time-honored laws, learned and observed during a century of living, that I would like to share with you in *Heart of the Matter*.

PART 1

LAWS FOR FULFILLING YOUR LIFE'S MISSION

CHAPTER 1

BEGIN WITH THE END IN MIND

Do not take even one step in a direction you do not want to go.

I have long seen the wisdom of beginning with the end in mind. This truth became clear during my surgical training. No surgeon begins an operation without plans to close the wound at the end of the procedure. In fact, I never began an operation without making sure the instruments for closing the incision were on the table in the precise sequence I needed them.

Beginning with the end in mind is a principle that applies in countless applications. When a farmer plants crops, he envisions the harvest. When a pilot directs an airplane down the runway, she knows where she intends to land. When a contractor turns the first spade of earth, he does so from a blueprint that tells him what the structure will look like when completed. Beginning with the end in mind is vital to any task.

It is also a divine principle. For "where there is no vision, the people perish."[1]

Our Heavenly Father has been clear about *His* vision: "For behold, this is my work and my glory—to bring to pass the immortality and eternal life of man."[2] Jesus Christ left no doubt about the reason He condescended to come to this earth: "For I came down from heaven, not to do mine own will, but the will of him that sent me."[3]

Beginning with the end in mind literally affects everything we do. It helps us set our course, outline the steps to get there, and monitor our progress along the way. Having a vision of where we are headed makes the chances of getting there infinitely more likely.

What Is the "End" of Church Membership?

For years now, I have taught missionaries that their purpose is not to see how many people they can help join the Church. There is no point in baptizing and confirming someone if he or she is going to stop living as a Latter-day Saint after making his or her first covenant with God. The goal of missionaries is to teach all who will listen about life eternal and how to qualify for it. This means, of course, teaching about the blessings of the temple.

Those who step onto the covenant path and continue to progress along that path enjoy the "blessed and happy state of those that keep the commandments of God. For behold, they are blessed in all things, both temporal and spiritual; and if they hold out faithful to the end they are received into heaven, that thereby they may dwell with God in a state of never-ending happiness."[4]

Never-ending happiness is the goal. *Following the path that leads to never-ending happiness is the epitome of beginning with the end in mind.*

I feel strongly enough about this principle that on January 16, 2018, when I delivered my first message as President of the Church, I did so from the Salt Lake Temple annex. The context *was* the message. I wanted to be with each member of the Lord's Church *in* the house of the Lord.

In my brief message, I focused on the blessings of the temple and invited each member of the Church to begin with the end in mind. I also invited them to be endowed in the house of the Lord, sealed as families, and faithful to their temple covenants.

Then, just three months into my presidency, I undertook an around-the-world ministry trip with my wife, Wendy, and Elder Jeffrey R. Holland and Sister Patricia Holland. Each stop on that lengthy tour had a significant tie to the temple. In Jerusalem, we spoke about the importance of ancient temples and the temple the Savior loved. In Kenya, Zimbabwe, India, and Thailand, we referred to the temples that had been announced for their areas. In London, Hong Kong, and Laie, Hawaii, we referred to the blessings of the historically significant temples in each of those locations.[5]

Surely, for each of us, the "end" we would most like to achieve is to live forever with our families in an exalted state where we will be in the presence of God, our Heavenly Father, and His Son Jesus Christ. The temple marks the path that leads there. Staying on the covenant path opens the door to every spiritual blessing our Father has for His children.

Parable of the Bee and the Butter

One warm summer night, Wendy and I were having dinner on our patio when a pesky bee kept buzzing around us. Though I repeatedly waved a napkin at the bee, he persisted and was fascinated with our butter. We finally gave up trying to shoo him away and watched him land on the butter and gorge himself.

Moments later he was dead. In a matter of minutes, this energetic bee progressed from temptation to indulgence and then to death. He succumbed to a distraction that trapped and then destroyed him.

The lesson is obvious. Your ultimate safety lies in never taking even the first enticing step in a direction you do not want to go. Do you really want to end up where that first wrong step will lead you? The bee did not want to die. So be careful. Ask yourself when you are taking a first step: "Do I really want the end result of this choice I'm tempted to make?" Every addiction begins with drinking or smoking or watching something that leads to danger and a loss of agency. What may seem like a harmless flirtation can result in a tragic end. Avoid unnecessary tragedies in your life by refusing to take the first step down a forbidden path. If I were talking with you, I would repeat that last sentence.

On the other hand, beginning with the end in mind can lead to positive outcomes. I think of a grandson who, upon graduating from high school, asked how many years of schooling it would take to become a heart surgeon. When I told him that it would take about fourteen more years, he said, "Oh, that's too long, Grandfather." I then asked him how old he would be in fourteen years if he did *not* pursue his dream of becoming a heart surgeon. He got the message.

When he finished his training at the Mayo Clinic, it had indeed taken him fourteen years to become a heart surgeon. Because he pursued his education with the end in mind, he achieved his dream.

Beginning with the end in mind can help in almost any situation. As one simple example, whenever I anticipate greeting a dignitary who will be meeting with the First Presidency, I review pertinent details such as my most recent visit to his or her country to help me engage in a meaningful conversation with our guest. I want him or her to feel completely welcome and to leave feeling that life is better because of our time together. So, I picture, plan, and prepare for that desired outcome.

As you begin with the end in mind, you will accomplish more and avoid unnecessary disasters.

Envisioning a Goal Makes a Difference

Many years ago, I was invited to be a visiting professor of surgery in the People's Republic of China. Upon meeting and becoming well acquainted with my host, Dr. Zhang, I found myself picturing him in white baptismal clothing. Then, when I met Dr. Zhang's wife, I couldn't help but think of the two of them dressed in white in the temple together. I realized these thoughts were not practical, as I was not permitted to talk about the gospel while in China and I strictly adhered to that rule. Nonetheless, over the course of many trips to China, Dr. Zhang and I became dear friends.

Six years after my call to the Quorum of the Twelve Apostles, I received an unexpected letter from Dr. Zhang. He said that he had lived under both Japanese and Chinese rule and had also worked in a Presbyterian hospital. Then he said that he was now seventy years old, and the only way of living that made sense to him was Dr. Russell Nelson's. He wanted to know if he could be taught the gospel if he and his wife moved to Toronto, Canada. I of course told him that I would be delighted to arrange for him to meet with missionaries.

A few weeks after contacting the mission president in Toronto, I learned that these dear friends were ready to be baptized. I flew to Toronto to participate in their baptismal service. After their confirmations, I told them that I would return in one year to perform their sealing as a couple in the Toronto Ontario Temple, which I did. These were singular treasured experiences that commenced by visualizing them dressed in white.

For What Do You Want to Be Known?

The most crucial questions we should ask ourselves are simple ones: How will we choose to live our lives? And what kind of lives do we want to live forever?

The Lord explained the purpose of this mortal life to Abraham: "And we will prove them [meaning each one of us] herewith, to see if they will do all things whatsoever the Lord their God shall command them; And they who keep their first estate [premortality] shall be added upon; and they who keep not their first estate shall not have glory in the same kingdom with those who keep their first estate; and they who keep their second estate shall have glory added upon their heads for ever and ever."[6]

Our "second estate" is mortality, the life we are now living. As the Apostle Paul wrote in his epistle to Titus, the glory promised us is the "hope of eternal life, which God . . . promised before the world began."[7]

One of the primary things I have learned in a century of living is that what we do here on earth matters! How we choose to live our lives really matters! The notion that we should "eat, drink, and be merry, for tomorrow we die; and it shall be well with us"[8] is one of the most absurd lies in the universe.

At the end of this life, for what would you like to be known? I hope it will be said of me that . . .

I rendered service to my fellow man.

I had a family comprised of good people trying to do their best.

I demonstrated unshakable faith in God and lived accordingly.

I was kind to others and made the world a better place.

I kept my covenants.

The highest compliment you or I can receive is that we are covenant-keepers.

The honors of men, as exhilarating as they may seem at the time, fade quickly—especially when compared to what the Lord has in store for His covenant-keeping children.

This Life Will Not Last Forever

Several times in my life, I have come face-to-face with death. One of those occurred in Maputo, Mozambique, in late May 2009. While dining at the mission home there with Elder William W. Parmley, the Africa Southeast Area President, and his wife, Shanna, and with Mozambique Maputo Mission president, Blair J. Packard, and his wife Cindy, three men armed with automatic weapons burst into the room.

In the melee that followed, one robber put a gun to my head, announced they were there to kill me and abduct my wife, and then pulled the trigger. The gun made a clicking sound but did not fire. The misfire infuriated the robber, who then kicked me in the face and knocked me to the floor. I was certain that this was the end for me. I remember thinking, "I am about to pass out of this life and go into the next. This is going to be a very interesting experience."

At the same time, another robber shoved a pistol into Wendy's back and began rocking her chair in an attempt to pull her from it, saying, "You are coming with us! You are coming with us!"

Through a series of miraculous events—and thanks in no small part to the heroic actions of Sister Cindy Packard—our lives were spared. However, as I had on several previous frightening occasions, I realized how fragile life is and how relatively few things there are in this world that have eternal significance. As those robbers threatened our lives, I was not thinking about awards or educational degrees or commendations. I was thinking about my family and the covenants I had made with the Lord.

I fear that too many of us are living our lives as though this life is all there is, that life will not continue after death, and that what we do here has no bearing on the future. That is simply not true.

It is imperative that we not get distracted and pulled off the covenant path by the world's "shiny objects," meaning the honors and attention of men. Those events are of no importance whatsoever in the next world. What *will* matter is if we have made covenants with God and kept them.

It will also matter if we have been able to find joy in the journey and if we have helped others experience joy as well.

Joy Helps Us See the End from the Beginning

Finding and seeing the joy in our lives can change the very way we look at everything that happens—including the difficult moments.

These are the latter days, so none of us should be surprised when we see prophecy fulfilled. A host of prophets, including Isaiah, Paul, Nephi, and Mormon, foresaw that perilous times would come,[9] that in our day the whole world would be in commotion,[10] that men would be "lovers of pleasures more than lovers of God,"[11] and that many would become servants of Satan and uphold the adversary's work.[12] Indeed, you and I "wrestle . . . against the rulers of the darkness of this world, [and] against spiritual wickedness in high places."[13]

As conflicts between nations escalate, terrorists prey on the innocent, and corruption in everything from business to government becomes increasingly commonplace, what can help us?

The prophet Lehi taught a principle for spiritual survival that goes hand in hand with the concept of beginning with the end in mind. First, consider his circumstances: He had been persecuted for preaching truth in Jerusalem and commanded by the Lord to leave his possessions and flee with his family into the wilderness. Life was not at all ideal. He was living in a tent while watching two of his sons rebel against the teachings of the Lord and attack their younger brothers.

Lehi knew opposition, anxiety, heartache, pain, disappointment, and sorrow. Yet he declared, "Men are, that they might have joy."[14]

Life is filled with detours and dead ends, trials and challenges of every kind. Each of us has likely experienced times when distress, anguish, and despair have almost consumed us. Yet we are here to have joy?

Yes! The answer is a resounding yes! But how is that possible? What can we do to claim the joy that Heavenly Father has in store for us?

Eliza R. Snow, second General President of the Relief Society, offered a riveting example of this very thing. Because of Missouri's infamous extermination order issued at the onset of the grueling winter of 1838,[15] she and other Saints were forced to flee the state that winter. One evening, Eliza's family spent the night in a small log cabin used by refugee Saints. Much of the chinking between the logs had been extracted and burned for firewood by those who preceded them. There were holes between the logs large enough for a cat to crawl through. It was bitter cold, and their food was frozen solid.

That night some eighty people huddled inside that small cabin. Most sat or stood all night trying to keep warm. Outside, a group of men spent the night gathered around a roaring fire. Eliza recorded: "Not a complaint was heard—all were cheerful, and judging from appearances, strangers would have taken us to be pleasure excursionists rather than a band of gubernatorial exiles."

Eliza said of their bone-numbing evening: "That was a very merry night. None but saints can be happy under every circumstance."[16]

Eliza R. Snow, and those with her, surely had their focus fixed on their end goal: staying true to their faith and to the Lord. She said it well: "Saints can be happy under every circumstance." We can feel joy even while having a bad day, a bad week, or a bad year!

The joy we feel has little to do with the circumstances of our lives and everything to do with the focus of our lives!

When the focus of our lives is on God's plan of salvation and Jesus Christ and His gospel, we can feel joy regardless of what is happening—or not happening—in our lives. Jesus Christ is the source of all joy. For Latter-day Saints, Jesus Christ *is* joy!

The Savior offers peace that "passeth all understanding."[17] Wendy and I experienced the Savior's peace during that frightening experience in Mozambique. It did not make sense to feel at peace in the midst of guns and threats to our lives. And yet, we did.

So, too, Jesus Christ offers an intensity, depth, and breadth of joy that defies human logic. For example, it does not seem possible to feel joy when your child suffers with an incurable illness or when you lose your job or when your spouse betrays you. Yet that is precisely the joy the Savior offers to all who have their focus fixed on Him, to all who are proceeding forward with the glorious end of eternal life in mind. The Savior's joy is constant, assuring us that our "afflictions shall be but a small moment"[18] and shall be consecrated for our gain.[19]

How Can We Claim Joy and Keep the End in Mind?

How can we claim joy and keep the end in mind during difficult times?

We can start by "looking unto Jesus the author and finisher of our faith."[20] As the Savior becomes more and more real to us, and as we plead for His joy to be given to us, our joy will increase and our end goal will seem increasingly achievable.

Joy is powerful, and focusing on joy brings God's power into our lives. As in all things, Jesus Christ is our ultimate exemplar—"who for the joy that was set before him endured the cross."[21] Imagine! In order to endure the most excruciating experience on this earth, our Savior focused on joy! The joy of doing His Father's will. The joy of doing what He came here to do, including the joy of healing us from sadness, loneliness, and fear; the joy of strengthening us during difficult times; the joy of paying for the sins of all who would repent; the joy of making it possible for you and me to return home—clean and worthy—to live with our Heavenly Parents and families.

As we follow our Savior's pattern and focus on the joy that will come to us, and to those we love, we can endure the challenges that presently seem overwhelming, painful, scary, and unfair.

Consider for a moment what you and I will be able to endure as we focus on the joy that is "set before us." What repenting will then be possible? What weakness will become a strength?[22] What disappointments, even tragedies, will turn to our good?[23] What challenging service to the Lord will we be able to give?[24]

When we focus on our eventual end goal, that of eternal life with our family in the presence of our Heavenly Parents and the Savior, staying on the covenant path will become easier. What we will achieve, overcome, and become will astonish us.

Avoid Those Things That Interrupt Joy

As we focus on the Savior and our eternal future, we need to avoid those things that can interrupt our joy. We need to avoid anything that would prevent us from keeping the end in mind.

Remember Korihor, the anti-Christ? Spewing falsehoods about

the Savior, Korihor went from place to place until he was brought before a high priest who asked him: "Why do ye teach this people that there shall be no Christ, to *interrupt their rejoicings*?"[25] The Book of Mormon is filled with examples of men and women who experience joy and rejoicing because they chose to follow Jesus Christ. Any other choice, as in the case of Korihor, leads to eventual destruction.

Anything that opposes Christ or His doctrine will interrupt our joy and take our focus off our end goal. Beware of the philosophies of men, which are so abundant online and throughout social media.

The world teaches that the purchase of things will bring joy. And if that doesn't work, buy more! It teaches that you can sin your way to joy. And if that doesn't work, sin more! It promises a pot of joy at the end of every hedonistic rainbow. But these philosophies are simply not true.

The unrighteous may experience any number of emotions and sensations, but they will never experience joy! Not in this world or in the world to come. *Joy is a gift for the faithful.* Those who keep eternal life uppermost in mind, and keep their covenants, are those who "shall inherit the kingdom of God, . . . and their joy shall be full forever."[26]

Joy is the gift that comes from intentionally trying to live a righteous life, as taught by Jesus Christ.[27]

As this truth is embedded in our hearts, each day can be a day of joy and gladness. Each day can take us one step closer to our ultimate goal: to qualify for the greatest gift of God, the gift of eternal life.

CHAPTER 2

DISCOVER THE POWER OF DIVINE LAW

Divine law is irrefutable whereas relative truth is rarely true.

Many decades ago, I visited Havana, Cuba, as a tourist and contracted the services of an English-speaking guide, George, to help our group while we were there. As George drove us around Havana to see the sights, a policeman pulled our vehicle over. An animated discussion ensued between George and the officer until George opened his wallet and handed several bills to the officer. The policeman drove away, and we resumed our sightseeing. When the opportunity presented itself, we asked George why he had been detained.

He responded with some indignation: "You folks from the United States are all alike," he said. "You don't understand or appreciate the liberty you have. You live in a land governed by law, and those laws are what give you freedom. Here in Havana, our society is regulated by the whims of men. If I want to survive as a tour guide, I have no choice but to submit to requests of the police, even when I have done nothing wrong. The police officer simply told me that if

I wanted to continue to be your guide, I would have to pay him for the privilege."

George articulated an important truth. Laws keep us free. Laws safeguard rather than restrict. Picture something as simple as a stop sign. How many accidents, including collisions resulting in serious injury or even death, does just one stop sign prevent in one day's time? Laws both protect us and give us freedom.

I can see two stoplights from the windows in my home. Sometimes when I cannot sleep, I glance out at the street and am fascinated to see a random driver stopping at a stoplight at 2:00 a.m., even though no other cars are on the road and no police are in the area. I love living in a country where most of the citizens, most of the time, obey the law of their own accord. I have traveled in many countries where a stop sign is simply a suggestion. I have learned that the rule of law is the foundation for living in communities of justice, opportunity, and peace.

That being said, even the finest man-made laws cannot compare with God's laws, or divine truths, that also govern our lives—whether we realize it or not.

I was reminded of this a few years ago when my wife Wendy and I had occasion to visit a dear friend, a government official in another land whom I had known and respected for many years. It had been more than a year since we had seen each other, and I was caught off guard when an aide wheeled him into our meeting in a wheelchair.

"I have been ill for quite some time," he explained. "But I wanted to see you again." As he reflected about his life, he told us what had been occupying his mind. "Most days I lie in my bed, look up at the ceiling, and ask myself, 'What is true?'"

My friend's age and impending death had turned his attention to one of life's greatest questions: What is true?

What Is True?

I asked myself the same question again and again during my medical training, and particularly during my internship and residency. During those early days of surgical training, I found myself in the middle of a burgeoning new field of medical research. As I mentioned in the Introduction, in medical school, I had been taught that a doctor must never touch the human heart or it would stop beating. We were even warned that any doctor who attempted to touch the heart would lose credibility among his or her peers. At the time, that was the "truth" we believed about the heart.

But then, during my residency, I began working with a team developing an artificial heart-lung machine. I still remember vividly our first experiments on animals during which we bravely dared to open the chest and the pericardium, or sac around the heart. We did this only after injecting Novocain to anesthetize the heart so that it "would not know we were coming." Lo and behold, that experiment worked! We quickly learned that the heart would continue to function even if we did not "anesthetize" it. Contrary to the "truth" we had been taught in medical school, the heart continued to beat if we touched it, held it, and even cut into and stitched it!

So, we continued our quest to uncover more truths about the heart. We found that if we simply altered the sodium/potassium ratio in the blood that flows into the coronary arteries, the heart would stop beating instantly. Very literally, we could "turn the heart off" long enough to repair it. In order to perform certain operations, the heart must be still. One cannot splice spaghetti in motion. This success, however, raised an obvious question: Could we turn the heart back on again?

Further research answered that question. When we washed the potassium out with normal blood, the heart sprang back to life because we had restored the heart's normal sodium/potassium ratio. This same process—with many refinements over time, of course—is basically what surgeons use today to turn the heartbeat off and on, allowing for delicate surgical repairs.

In 1949 our team of researchers reported to the American College of Surgeons that, for the first time ever, an artificial heart-lung machine had sustained the life of an animal for thirty minutes! This was a major medical milestone. We eagerly shared the truths, or divine laws, related to the heart that we had discovered.

Long after my career as a heart surgeon had concluded, the dean of a prestigious medical school invited me to speak to their students. After I described the process we had gone through to learn how to turn the heartbeat off and on, the dean asked, "But what if it doesn't work?" I responded, simply, "It *always* works! This procedure is based on divine law, and divine law is irrefutable!"

Uncovering Divine Laws

During those early days of research on the heart, I came across some verses in the Doctrine and Covenants that resulted in a major epiphany for me, opening my mind to new possibilities for my heart research.

The first verses that caught my attention declared that "all kingdoms have a law given; And there are many kingdoms; for there is no space in the which there is no kingdom; and there is no kingdom in which there is no space, . . . And unto every kingdom is given a law; and unto every law there are certain bounds also and conditions."[1] The third verse builds upon the first two by saying that "when we obtain any blessing from God, it is by obedience to that law upon which it is predicated."[2]

When I read these verses in tandem, my young research-focused mind exploded with possibilities. "Surely," I thought, "there must be laws, or truths, that govern the beating heart." If we could discover those laws and then "obey" them, the results would be positive. It was the very idea that absolute truths, or divine laws, exist—and that following them would produce desirable results—that gave me new hope about discovering ways to repair a defective heart.

Further, I realized that whenever a blessing is received, it is because a law has been obeyed. This means certain procedures will always work—not some of the time, but *every time* without exception. Likening the scriptures to my field of interest greatly spurred my thinking relative to heart surgery.

The arbiter of truth is God—not your social media feed, your favorite podcaster, or even Google! None of us have the capacity to *create* truth. What we can do, however, is *discover* truth.

Divine Laws and Absolute Truths Never Change

There are absolute truths, and there are relative truths. Relative truths often change as science and discovery produce knowledge heretofore unknown. Relative truths can also change as a result of personal opinion.

But absolute truths never change. Gravity is an absolute truth. Gravity never varies. The fact that the earth is round is an absolute truth. The fact that the sum of the three angles of *any* triangle is always 180 degrees is an absolute truth. The fact that we were each born of a woman and that we will each eventually die are absolute truths.

Absolute truths are completely reliable, even incontrovertible. They do not change. This means that procedures and practices based on divine laws will work every time.

If they didn't, we would be afraid to climb into an airplane.

How would we know if the airplane would fly *this time*? But today, tens of thousands of passengers around the world board thousands of flights a day because we know there are divine laws that, when obeyed, give an airplane lift. These laws of aerodynamics allow a plane to take off, fly, and land safely. Neither doctors nor pilots have the power to *change* the laws that govern their professions, but their understanding and utilization of those laws save lives every day.

The Fallacy of Relative Truth

Today, relativism—the notion that knowledge, truth, and morality exist in relation to culture, society, and historical context—is widely accepted. Many find absolute truths inconvenient and claim there are no such things, that all truth is relative. They treat absolute truth like a fairy tale and assert that whatever you believe is "your truth" and whatever I believe is "my truth." But nothing could be further from *the* truth.

There is a difference between right and wrong. Truth is based upon the laws God has established for the protection and nurturing of His children. Divine laws operate in and affect each of our lives, whether we believe they do or not.

In the 1950s, when open-heart surgery on humans was in its infancy, I scheduled only one such operation a month. Frankly, each operation was a skirmish with terror. Every time we opened the heart, we came face-to-face with the unknown as well as with the limitations imposed by our sheer lack of knowledge. During almost every operation, we encountered something we had never encountered before. Those were days of true pioneering.

Such life-and-death confrontations forced us to return to the laboratory, do further research, and attempt to learn how to address the challenges we had uncovered during the previous operation.

After we had fortified ourselves by solving a specific problem, we would enter the whirlpool of another operative experience.

Truth was there all the time. It was absolute. But we had to discover it. As we identified absolute truths related to diagnosing heart disease and repairing the heart, we became increasingly able to help our patients not only survive an operation but thrive thereafter.

Absolute Truths Are Stabilizing

Divine law is reassuring. It gives us a firm foundation upon which to stand and provides a sense of security, because absolute truth is completely dependable. If you adhere to the laws or truths that govern any particular behavior, discipline, or activity, you will achieve the outcomes you desire.

Jesus Christ admonished us to "know the truth, and the truth shall make you free."[3] Truth literally frees us from the bondage of ignorance and fear! What could be more liberating than that?

Countless heroic men and women through the ages have been driven to discover truth and have blazed trails that have blessed us all. Sir Isaac Newton not only famously discovered gravity but was responsible for working out many of the principles of visible light and the laws of motion. It would be impossible to calculate how many modern conveniences are dependent upon the absolute truths he uncovered.

Where would we be without Thomas Edison, who expanded our understanding of electric power generation, mass communication, and sound recording? Or Michael Faraday, who made discoveries that led to the first electric motors and generators? Or James Watson and Francis Crick, who discovered the double-helix structure of DNA? Now researchers better understand the endless chemical patterns that create instructions for the human body—such as the color of our eyes and hair. This advancement is helping scientists today discover how to prevent diseases that were previously fatal.

The discovery of these and countless other absolute truths, or divine laws, have literally changed our lives.

Science and Religion Are Compatible

In many respects, what I learned as a heart surgeon is not much different from what I learned at church—that whenever I obey divine law, I am blessed. Or, said another way, whenever I adhere to divine laws or truths, I can depend on the outcome.

I have always been fascinated by those who claim that science and religion are at odds. In my experience, science and religion are beautifully compatible disciplines. Scientific research is nothing more or less than the effort to discover laws, or absolute truths, that God has already put in place. This is why truth is not relative. Truth is not based on your version of truth or my version of truth.

The only thing that is relative is our individual understanding of truth.

Divine Laws Are a Gift

Divine laws are God's gifts to His children. The Prophet Joseph Smith taught that God "institute[d] laws whereby [we] could have a privilege to advance like himself."[4]

President Spencer W. Kimball spoke about truth this way: "God, our Heavenly Father—Elohim—lives. That is an absolute truth. . . . All the people on the earth might deny him and disbelieve, but he lives in spite of them. . . . Opinion alone has no power in the matter of an absolute truth. He still lives. And Jesus Christ is the Son of God, the Almighty, the Creator, the Master of the only true way of life—the gospel of Jesus Christ. The intellectual may rationalize him out of existence and the unbeliever may scoff, but Christ still lives and guides the destinies of his people. That is an absolute truth; there is no gainsaying."[5]

President Kimball also taught that absolute truth cannot be "altered by the opinions of men. . . . If men are really humble, they will realize that they *discover*, but do not *create*, truth."[6]

As the prophet Jacob said, "The Spirit speaketh the truth and lieth not. Wherefore, it speaketh of things as they really are, and of things as they really will be."[7] The challenge for each of us, then, is to understand the truths of the gospel of Jesus Christ so that we can implement those truths in our lives.

Existentialists can expound; relativists can rationalize with their constricted views of reality. But laws are laws. I have no question whatsoever that there are divine laws that control the universe. When we obey God's laws, blessings follow. When we deny and abuse those laws, there are consequences.

Every major religion of which I am aware teaches that there is an absolute right and wrong. Moral relativism does not lead to order in society or in an individual life. Basing your life on relative truth will almost certainly lead to anxiety, because you cannot feel secure building your life on a foundation that shifts from one day or one year to the next.

Building your life upon relative truth calls to mind the oft-quoted parable in which Jesus drew a stark distinction between the wise man, who built his house upon the rock, and the foolish man, who built upon the sand. "And the rain descended, and the floods came, and the winds blew, and beat upon that house; and it fell: and great was the fall of it."[8]

There are few things more unsettling than having the ground move beneath our feet. We were just a few days into shutdowns imposed by the COVID-19 pandemic when a 5.8-magnitude earthquake hit Salt Lake City. Buildings rocked and nerves frayed as the earth moved.

Choosing to live a life based upon shifting values and relative truths is deciding to live a life filled with emotional, intellectual, and spiritual earthquakes.

Seek to Discern Truth

Many years ago, I was serving—at some personal sacrifice—as a consultant to the U.S. government at its national Centers for Disease Control and Prevention in Atlanta, Georgia. On one trip there, after a long day of meetings, I was waiting outside for a taxi to take me to the airport. It was a beautiful, sunny January day, and I stretched out on the lawn to soak in a few welcome rays before returning to the wintry January weather of Utah. Later I received a photograph in the mail that captured my moment of relaxation on the lawn. Under it was the caption: "Governmental consultant at the National Center." Both the picture and caption were, strictly speaking, factual, but the photographer's conclusion couldn't have been further from the truth.

I invite you to make seeking for and understanding truth a lifelong quest. I invite you to find absolute truths upon which you can build a firm foundation for your life.

The existence of God, as our Heavenly Father, is an absolute truth.

The divinity of His Son, Jesus Christ, is an absolute truth. The reality of the Holy Ghost and His mission to bear witness of the Father and the Son and to testify of truth is an absolute truth. The presence and influence of these three members of the Godhead in our lives and Their willingness to bless and help us is an absolute truth. The fact that the gospel of Jesus Christ has been restored to the earth and is here in its fullness is an absolute truth.

These truths have anchored my life and given it a sense of profound meaning and purpose.

I return to my aged friend who knew his days in this life were coming to an end. The prevailing question in his mind was, "What is true?"

My plea is to seek truth long before the end to your mortal life is near. When you base your life upon absolute truth and divine law, then, when the metaphorical rains descend and the floods come and the winds blow, your house will not fall, because it is built upon the rock of truth.

CHAPTER 3

UNDERSTAND THE EVERLASTING COVENANT

Making covenants with God changes our relationship with Him forever.

I have spoken frequently about the importance of the Abrahamic covenant and the gathering of Israel. When we embrace the gospel and are baptized, we take upon ourselves the sacred name of Jesus Christ. We become joint-heirs to *all* the promises given anciently by the Lord to Abraham, Isaac, Jacob, and their posterity.[1]

The new and everlasting covenant and the Abrahamic covenant are essentially the same—two ways of phrasing the covenant made by God with mortal men and women at different times.

The adjective *everlasting* denotes that this covenant existed even *before* the foundation of the world! The plan laid out in the Grand Council in Heaven included the sobering realization that we would all be cut off from God's presence. However, God's plan promised that He would provide a Savior who would overcome the consequences of the Fall.

God told Adam after his baptism: "Thou art after the order of him who was without beginning of days or end of years, from all eternity to all eternity. Behold, thou [Adam] art one in me, a son of God; and thus may all become my sons."[2]

Adam and Eve accepted the ordinance of baptism and began the process of being one with God. They had entered the covenant path.

When you and I enter that same path, we have a new way of life. We thereby enter a relationship with God that allows Him to bless and change us. The covenant path leads us back to Him. If we let God prevail in our lives, the covenant path will lead us closer and closer to Him. All covenants are intended to be binding. They create a relationship with everlasting ties.

The Significance of Covenants with God

Once we make a covenant with God, we leave neutral ground forever. God will not abandon His relationship with those who have forged such a bond with Him. In fact, all those who have made a covenant with God have access to a special kind of love and mercy. In the Hebrew language, that covenantal love is called *hesed* (חֶסֶד).[3]

Hesed has no adequate English equivalent. Translators of the King James Version of the Bible must have struggled with how to render *hesed* in English. They often chose "lovingkindness." This captures much but not all the meaning of *hesed*. Other translations were also rendered, such as "mercy" and "goodness." *Hesed* is a unique term describing a covenant relationship in which both parties are bound to be loyal and faithful to each other. For example, a celestial marriage is such a covenant relationship. *Hesed* is a special kind of love and mercy that God feels for and extends to those who have made a covenant with Him. And we reciprocate with *hesed* for Him.

Because God has *hesed* for those who have covenanted with Him, He will love them. He will continue to work with them and offer them opportunities to change. He will forgive them when they repent. And should they stray, He will help them find their way back to Him.

Once you and I have made a covenant with God, our relationship with Him becomes much closer than before our covenant. Now, we are bound together. Because of our covenant with God, He will *never tire* in His efforts to help us, and we will never exhaust His merciful patience with us. Each of us has a special place in God's heart. He has high hopes for us.

The Lord made a historic declaration to the Prophet Joseph Smith by revelation: "This promise is yours also, because ye are of Abraham, and the promise was made unto Abraham."[4]

Thereby, this everlasting covenant was restored as part of the great Restoration of the gospel in its fullness. Think of it! A marriage covenant made in the temple is tied directly to that Abrahamic covenant. There, a couple is introduced to *all* the blessings reserved for the faithful posterity of Abraham, Isaac, and Jacob.

Entering the Covenant Path

As did Adam, you and I personally entered the covenant path at baptism. We then enter it more completely in the temple. The blessings of the Abrahamic covenant are conferred in holy temples. These blessings allow us to inherit thrones, kingdoms, powers, principalities, and dominions, to our "exaltation and glory in all things,"[5] when we are resurrected.

In the closing text of the Old Testament, we read of Malachi's promise that Elijah will "turn the heart of the fathers to the children, and the heart of the children to their fathers."[6] In ancient Israel, such reference to the fathers would have included our fathers Abraham, Isaac, and Jacob. This promise is clarified when we read the different version of this verse that Moroni quoted to the Prophet Joseph Smith: "He [Elijah] shall plant in the hearts of the children the promises made to the fathers, and the hearts of the children shall turn to their fathers."[7] Those fathers surely include Abraham, Isaac, and Jacob.

Christ's atoning sacrifice enabled the Father to fulfill His promises made to His children. Because Jesus Christ is "the way, the truth, and the life," it follows that "no man cometh unto the Father, but by [Him]."[8] The fulfillment of the Abrahamic covenant becomes feasible because of the Atonement of our Savior, the Lord Jesus Christ. Jesus Christ is at the *center* of the Abrahamic covenant.

The Old Testament is not only a book of scripture; it is a book of history. You remember studying the marriage of Sarai and Abram.[9] As they were childless,[10] Sarai gave her handmaid, Hagar, to be Abram's wife also.[11] Hagar gave birth to Ishmael.[12] Abram loved Ishmael, but he was not to be the child through whom the covenant would pass.

As a blessing from God, and in response to Sarai's faith,[13] she conceived in her advanced years so that the covenant would pass through *her* son, Isaac.[14] He was born in the covenant. God gave Sarai and Abram new names—*Sarah* and *Abraham*.[15] The bestowal of those new names marked the beginning of a new life and a new destiny for this family.

Abraham loved both Ishmael and Isaac. God told Abraham that Ishmael would be multiplied and become a great nation.[16] At the same time, God made it clear that the everlasting covenant would be established through Isaac.[17]

All who accept the gospel become part of the lineage of Abraham: "For as many of you as have been baptized into Christ have put on Christ. . . . Ye are all one in Christ Jesus. And if ye be Christ's, then are ye Abraham's seed, and heirs according to the promise."[18]

Thus, we too can become heirs to the covenant either by birth or by adoption. Isaac and Rebekah's son Jacob was born in the covenant. In addition, he chose to enter the everlasting covenant of his own accord. As you know, Jacob's name was changed to *Israel,* meaning "let God prevail," or "God prevails."[19] We will discuss this further in chapter 17.

In Exodus 2:24, we read that "God remembered his covenant with Abraham, with Isaac, and with Jacob." God told the children of Israel: "If ye will obey my voice indeed, and keep my covenant, then ye shall be a peculiar treasure unto me."[20] The phrase "peculiar treasure" was translated from the Hebrew *segullah,* meaning "highly valued possession—a treasure."

The Importance of the Everlasting Covenant

The book of Deuteronomy recounts the importance of the covenant. Apostles of the New Testament knew of this covenant. When Peter healed a lame man on the temple steps, he taught onlookers about Jesus. Peter said, "The God of Abraham, and of Isaac, and of Jacob, the God of our fathers, hath glorified his Son Jesus."[21]

Peter closed his message by telling his audience that "ye are the children of the prophets, and of the covenant which God made with our fathers, saying unto Abraham, And in thy seed shall all the kindreds of the earth be blessed."[22] Peter made it clear that part of Christ's mission was to fulfill God's covenant.

A similar sermon was given by the Lord to the people of ancient America. There, the resurrected Christ told the people who they really were. He said: "Ye are the children of the prophets; and ye are of the house of Israel; and ye are of the covenant which the Father made with your fathers, saying unto Abraham: And in thy seed shall all the kindreds of the earth be blessed. The Father having raised me up unto you first, and sent me to bless you in turning away every one of you from [your] iniquities; and this because ye are the children of the covenant."[23]

The significance of this is profound! Those who keep their covenants with God will become a strain of sin-resistant souls who have the desire and strength to overcome the world!

God has commanded that we spread the great news of the gospel and share the covenant. He wishes for every one of His children to have the opportunity to choose the Savior's gospel and embark upon the covenant path. God wants to connect *all people* to the covenant He made anciently with Abraham. Thus, missionary work is an essential part of the great gathering of Israel.

But there is even more—much more. There is a huge need to spread the gospel to people on the other side of the veil. God wants everyone, on both sides of the veil, to enjoy the blessings of His covenant. The covenant path is open to all. We plead with everyone to walk that path with us. No other work is so universally inclusive. For "the Lord is merciful unto all who will, in the sincerity of their hearts, call upon his holy name."[24]

At the dedication of the Kirtland Temple in 1836, under the direction of the Lord, Elijah appeared. His purpose? "To turn the hearts of the fathers to the children, and turn the children to the fathers."[25] Elias also appeared. His purpose? To commit to Joseph Smith and Oliver Cowdery the keys of "the dispensation of the gospel of Abraham, saying that in us and our seed all generations after us should be blessed."[26] Thus, "the Master conferred upon Joseph [and Oliver] priesthood authority and the right to convey [the unique] blessings of the Abrahamic covenant to others."[27]

In the Church, we travel the covenant path both individually and collectively. Just as marriages and families share a unique *lateral* bond that creates a special love, so does the new relationship formed when we bind ourselves by covenant *vertically* to our God!

This is exactly why, as part of the covenant, a special mercy and love—or *hesed*—is available to all who enter this binding and intimate relationship with God, even to a thousand generations.[28]

Making a covenant with God changes our relationship with Him forever. It blesses us with an extra measure of love and mercy.[29] It affects who we are and how God will help us become what we can become.

Those who make sacred covenants and keep them are promised exaltation, "the greatest of all the gifts of God."[30] Jesus Christ is the guarantor of those covenants.[31] Covenant keepers who love God and allow Him to prevail over all other things in their lives make Him the most powerful influence in their lives.

Now, dear brothers and sisters, our callings in the Church are not calls to prominence. They are not calls to attract a following. They are calls to serve. They are calls to make sure every member realizes the joy and privileges associated with making covenants with God. They are calls to encourage every covenant-keeping man and woman, boy and girl, to be willing to share the gospel with those who come within their sphere of influence.

Every man and every woman who makes covenants with God and keeps them, and who participates in priesthood ordinances, has direct access to the power of God. Truly, every benevolent act of The Church of Jesus Christ of Latter-day Saints and its members is an expression of God's *hesed.*

The Covenant Path Is a Path of Love

Now, let us review a few key points.

Why was Israel scattered? Because the people broke the

commandments and stoned the prophets. A loving but grieving Father responded by scattering Israel far and wide. He promised, however, that one day Israel would be gathered again into His fold.

The tribe of Judah was given responsibility to prepare the world for the first coming of the Lord. From that tribe, Mary was called upon to be the mother of the Son of God.

The tribe of Joseph, through his and Asenath's[32] sons, Ephraim and Manasseh, was given the responsibility to lead in the gathering of Israel, to prepare the world for the Second Coming of the Lord.

In such a timeless *hesed* relationship, it is only natural that God wants to gather Israel. He is our Heavenly Father! He wants each of His children—on both sides of the veil—to hear the message of the restored gospel of Jesus Christ.

The covenant path is a path of love—that incredible *hesed*, that compassionate caring for and reaching out to each other. The greatest joy you will ever experience is when you are consumed with love for God and for all His children.

Loving God more than anyone or anything else is the condition that brings true peace, comfort, confidence, and joy.

The Book of Mormon begins and ends with reference to this everlasting covenant. From its title page to the closing testimonies of Mormon and Moroni, reference is made to the covenant.[33] "The coming forth of the Book of Mormon is a sign to the entire world that the Lord has commenced to gather Israel and fulfill the covenants He made to Abraham, Isaac, and Jacob."[34]

CHAPTER 4

UNDERSTAND WHO YOU ARE AND WHOSE YOU ARE

Make sure you see yourself as God does.

As a former medical student, researcher, and professor, I have spent a lot of time on campuses. I love any environment that stimulates learning. Education is important. In fact, I consider it a religious responsibility. "The glory of God is intelligence."[1]

There is a major difference, however, between the responsibilities of secular educators and my responsibility as the senior Apostle on earth. Their job is to educate and prepare their students for their *mortal* experience—meaning, how to succeed in their life's work. My responsibility is to educate and prepare you for your *immortal* experience—meaning, how to gain eternal life.

Teachings of the finest institutions of higher learning have limitations. Secular education generally ignores three major divine truths that are rarely addressed or even acknowledged:

1. First, each of us is going to die.[2]

2. Second, because of Jesus Christ, each of us is going to be resurrected and become immortal.[3]
3. And third, each of us will have a personal interview with the Savior during which we will be judged.[4]

These three absolute truths should form the foundation of your spiritual education.

Because of the Restoration of the gospel of Jesus Christ in its fullness, we know a lot about our postmortal possibilities. We know that our Father's house has many mansions.[5] We know that God loves His children so much that, as President Dallin H. Oaks taught, "*all the children of God*"—with the fewest of exceptions—will "wind up in a kingdom of *glory*."[6] Just think of it! Our Father created kingdoms of *glory*—telestial, terrestrial, and celestial—to provide a glorious place for His children. Jesus taught that "in my Father's house are many mansions."[7]

My purpose is to make sure that your eyes are *wide open* to the truth that this life really *is* the time when you get to decide what kind of life *you* want to live forever. Right now *is* your time "to prepare to meet God."[8] For all "shall be judged . . . , and every man shall receive according to *his* own works, *his* own dominion, in the mansions which are prepared."[9]

Mortal lifetime is barely a nanosecond compared with eternity. But what a crucial nanosecond it is! Consider carefully how it works: During this mortal life you get to choose which laws you are willing to obey—those of the celestial kingdom, or the terrestrial, or the telestial[10]—and, therefore, in which kingdom of glory you will live forever. What a plan! It is a plan that completely honors *your* agency.

Every righteous choice that you make here will pay huge dividends now and unimaginable dividends eternally. If you choose to make covenants with God and are faithful to those covenants, you have the promise of "glory added upon [your head] for ever and ever."[11]

These truths ought to prompt your ultimate sense of FOMO—or fear of missing out. The ultimate FOMO would be missing out on the celestial kingdom by settling for a lesser kingdom because here on earth you chose only to live the laws of a lesser kingdom.

Different kingdoms of glory have different requirements, with those for the celestial kingdom being the most rigorous. Each kingdom also has different privileges, with those of the celestial kingdom being the most grand and all-encompassing. Ironically, the Lord has not revealed very much about the telestial or terrestrial kingdoms. He has, however, told us a lot about the celestial kingdom, which is described in both the New Testament and the Doctrine and Covenants as having the "glory of the sun."[12]

Because of the glorious principle of agency, we each get to choose the kind of life we want to live eternally. Our eventual assignment to a kingdom of glory will be based largely on what we are willing to do in this life, the desires of our hearts, and what we "are willing to receive" from God.[13] For "he who is not able to abide the law of a celestial kingdom cannot abide a celestial glory."[14]

The adversary, of course, does not want you even to think about tomorrow, let alone eternal life. Please don't be uninformed or naive about the opportunities and challenges of mortality. In that spirit, please consider three fundamental truths that will help you prepare your future course:

1. First, know the truth about who you are.
2. Second, know the truth about what Heavenly Father and His Son have offered you.
3. And third, know the truth related to your own conversion to Jesus Christ and His restored gospel.

Know the Truth about Who You Are

I believe that the first thing the Lord wants you to understand is who you truly are!

This is exactly what He taught the people of ancient America when He spoke to them. After identifying who *He* was, He told His listeners who *they* were: "And behold, ye are the children of the prophets; and ye are of the house of Israel; and ye are of the covenant."[15]

These same truths were declared to people in biblical times. Peter taught that "ye are the children of the prophets, and of the covenant which God made with our fathers, saying unto Abraham, And in thy seed shall all the kindreds of the earth be blessed."[16]

You are literally a spirit child of God. You have no doubt sung this truth since you learned the words to "I Am a Child of God."[17] But is this eternal truth imprinted upon your heart?

Our young women and young men quote themes regularly that begin "I am a beloved daughter of heavenly parents, with a divine nature and eternity destiny" and "I am a beloved son of God, and He has a work for me to do."[18] But has this frequent repetition caused you to hear these truths so often that they now sound more like slogans than divine truth? This is an important question to consider, because the way you think about who you are affects every decision you will ever make.

Be Careful about Labels

In 2006, when I married Wendy, I was in for several surprises. One surprise was the number of clothing items she owned that displayed a logo—universities from which she had graduated, favorite places she had traveled, and so forth. Whenever she wore one of those items, I teased her by saying, "Who are you advertising today?" She invited me to join in the fun and made sure I had my own wardrobe with favorite logos!

Labels *can* be fun and indicate our support for any number of positive things. They can even evoke memories of important accomplishments and experiences. But not all labels are of equal value. If any label replaces our most important identifiers, the results can be spiritually deadly.

For example, if I were to rank in order of importance the designations that could be applied to me, I would say: First, I am a child of God—a son of God—then a son of the covenant, then a disciple of Jesus Christ and a devoted member of His restored Church.

Next would come my honored titles as a husband and father, then Apostle of the Lord Jesus Christ.

All other labels that have applied to me—such as a medical doctor, surgeon, researcher, professor, lieutenant, captain, PhD, American, and so forth—would fall somewhere down the list.

Now, let me turn the question to you. *Who are you?*

First and foremost, you are a child of God.

Second, if you are a member of the Church, you are a child of the covenant. When you were baptized, you made very specific covenants with the Lord. You promised to bear others' burdens, mourn with those that mourn, comfort those in need of comfort, and "stand as witnesses of God at all times and in all things."[19]

And third, you are a disciple of Jesus Christ.

I plead with you not to *replace* these three paramount and unchanging identifiers with any others, because doing so could stymie your progress or pigeonhole you into a stereotype that could potentially thwart your eternal progression.

For example, if you are identified mainly as an American, those who are not Americans may think, "I know everything there is to know about you because you are an American." Because of this erroneous assumption, they may assign erroneous attributes to you.

If you identify yourself by your political affiliation, you will instantly be categorized as having certain beliefs—though I don't know anyone who believes everything that their preferred political party presently embraces.

I could go on and on, rehearsing the constraints of various labels that we put on ourselves or that other people place upon us.

Some might label me as an "old man." But I'm a lot younger than Adam was—and Noah too.[20] Ageism, racism, nationalism, sexism, and a host of other "isms" are universally limiting and are to be avoided.

How tragic it is when someone believes the label another person has given them. Imagine the heartache of a child who is told, "You are dumb" or "You are ugly." Identifiers and labels are powerful!

The adversary rejoices in labels because they divide us and restrict the way we think about ourselves and each other. Labels can divide us into the kinds of tribes that divided the Nephites prior to the Lord's first coming.[21] Tribal divisions almost always lead to animosity, misunderstanding, and even tribal warfare. How limiting it is when we essentially "choose up sides." How sad it is when we honor labels more than we honor each other.

Labels almost inevitably lead to judging and animosity. Any abuse or prejudice toward another because of nationality, race, sexual orientation, gender, educational degrees, culture, or *any* other significant identifiers is offensive to our Maker! Such mistreatment causes us to live beneath our stature as His covenant sons and daughters!

There are various labels that may be very important to you, of course. Please do not misunderstand me. I am not saying that other designations and identifiers are not important. I am simply saying that no identifier should *displace*, *replace*, or *take priority over* the three paramount, enduring designations: "child of God," "child of the covenant," and "disciple of Jesus Christ."

Any identifier that is not compatible with these three basic designations will ultimately let you down. No other labels have the power to lead you toward eternal life in the celestial kingdom of God.

Worldly identifiers will *never* give you a vision of who you can ultimately become. They will never affirm your divine DNA or your unlimited, divine potential.

Because there is a grand plan of salvation authored by your Heavenly Father, you have a divine destiny.

President Orson Hyde, former President of the Quorum of the Twelve Apostles, said that "we understood things better [in the premortal world] than we do in this lower world." He continued, surmising about promises we likely made there: "It is not impossible that we signed the articles thereof with our own hands, which articles may be retained in the archives above, to be presented to us when we rise from the dead, and be judged out of our own mouths, according to that which is written in the books."[22]

Make no mistake about it: Your potential is divine. With your diligent seeking, God will give you glimpses of who you may become.

So, who are you? First and foremost, you are a child of God, a child of the covenant, and a disciple of Jesus Christ. As you embrace and live up to these truths, your Heavenly Father will help you reach your ultimate goal of living eternally in His holy presence.

What Have the Father and the Son Offered You?

God the Father and His Son Jesus Christ have offered you everything!

Heavenly Father's plan for His children allows you to live where and how He lives and ultimately to become more and more like

Him. His plan literally makes the richest blessings of all eternity available to you, including the potential for you to become "joint-heirs with Christ."[23]

God knows all and sees all. In all of eternity, no one will ever know you or care about you as much as He does. No one will ever be closer to you than He is. No one will ever understand your worries, concerns, and challenges like He does. You can pour out your heart to Him and trust Him to send the Holy Ghost and angels to care for you. He demonstrated His ultimate love when He sent His Only Begotten Son to die for you—to be your Savior and your Redeemer!

Through His Atonement, Jesus Christ overcame the world.[24] Therefore, He is "mighty to . . . cleanse [you] from all unrighteousness."[25] He will deliver you from your most excruciating circumstances in His own way and time. He will bless you with strength, patience, and peace far greater than you can muster on your own. The Lord is mighty to deliver you just as He delivered Nephi from the clutches of Laban.[26]

As you come unto the Lord in faith, He will guide, preserve, and protect you. He will heal your broken heart and comfort you in your distress.[27] He will give you access to His power. And He will make the impossible in your life become possible.

Jesus Christ is the only enduring source of hope, peace, and joy for you. Satan can never replicate any of these. And make no mistake about it—Satan will *never, ever* help you. His motive is to trap you in behaviors or activities that lead you further and further away from the light and mission of Jesus Christ. The adversary's goal is that you will ultimately be left utterly alone and bereft.

On the other hand, God's work and His glory is to bring about the "immortality and eternal life of man."[28] God will do everything He can, short of violating your agency, to help you not *miss out* on the greatest blessings in all eternity.

God has a special love for each person who makes a covenant with Him in the waters of baptism. This divine love deepens as we make additional covenants and keep them. Then at the end of mortal life, precious is the reunion of each covenant child with our Heavenly Father.[29]

God also cares *deeply* that all His children have an opportunity to hear the glad tidings of the restored gospel. Heavenly Father has sent His children to earth for more than six millennia. Most of these people have not yet received the ordinances that qualify them for eternal life. That is why temples are so significant. That is why the gathering of Israel on both sides of the veil is *the* most important cause on earth today. You have an essential role in this gathering. I thank you for your help.

This now leads to the third point.

Know the Truth about Your Own Conversion

The truth is that you must *own* your *own* conversion. No one else can do it for you.

May I invite you to consider a few questions? Do you want to feel peace about concerns that presently plague you? Do you want to know Jesus Christ better? Do you want to learn how His divine power can heal your wounds and weaknesses? Do you want to experience the sweet, soothing power of the Atonement of Jesus Christ working in your life?

If your answer to those four questions is "yes," that is evidence that you want to have a strong testimony of Jesus Christ and His restored gospel. I plead with you to take charge of your testimony. Work for it. Own it. Care for it. Nurture it so that it will grow. Feed it truth. Don't pollute it with the false philosophies of unbelieving men and women and then wonder why your testimony is waning.

Engage in daily, earnest, humble prayer. Nourish yourself in the words of ancient and modern prophets. Ask the Lord to teach you how to hear Him better. Spend more time in the temple and in family history work.

As you make your testimony your highest priority, watch for miracles to happen in your life.

If you have questions about the gospel and about your life—and I hope you do—seek answers with the fervent desire to believe. Learn all you can about the gospel by turning to truth-filled sources for guidance. We live in the dispensation when "nothing shall be withheld."[30] Thus, in time, the Lord will answer all of your questions.

In the meantime, immerse yourself in the rich reservoir of revelation we have at our fingertips. I promise that doing so will strengthen your testimony, even if some of your questions are not yet answered. Your sincere questions, asked in faith, will *always* lead to greater faith and more knowledge.

If friends and family should step away from the Church, continue to love them. It is not for you to judge another's choice any more than you deserve to be criticized for staying faithful.

Now, please understand this: Do not be led astray by those whose doubts may be fueled by things *you cannot see* in their lives. Most of all, let your skeptical friends see how much *you* love the Lord and His gospel. Surprise their doubting hearts with your believing heart!

As you take charge of your testimony and cause it to grow, you will become truly converted.[31] You will become a more potent instrument in the hands of God.

There is nothing happening on this earth more important than helping to gather Israel *for Him*. Let your Heavenly Father know that you want to help. Ask Him to put you to work in this glorious cause. And then stand back and marvel at what happens when you let God prevail in your life.

I bless you to know the truth about who you are and to treasure the truth about your glorious potential. I bless you to take charge of your own testimony. And I bless you to have the desire and strength to keep your covenants.

As you do, I promise that you will experience spiritual growth, freedom from fear, and a confidence that you can scarcely imagine. You will have the strength to have a positive influence far beyond your natural capacity. And I promise that your future will be more exhilarating than anything you can presently believe.

PART 2

LAWS FOR NURTURING ENDURING RELATIONSHIPS

CHAPTER 5

REJECT THE PLAGUE OF CONTENTION

Twenty-first-century animosity is as deadly as COVID-19.

During my surgical internship, I assisted a surgeon who was amputating a leg filled with highly infectious gangrene. The operation was difficult and taxing for everyone in the room. Then, to add to the tension, a member of the surgical team performed an important task poorly and the surgeon erupted in anger. In the middle of his tantrum, he threw his scalpel loaded with germs. Unfortunately, the scalpel landed in *my* forearm.

Everyone in the operating room—except the out-of-control surgeon, who seemed oblivious to his poor behavior—was horrified by this dangerous breach of surgical practice. Gratefully, I did not become infected. But the experience left a lasting impression on me. In that very hour, I promised myself that whatever happened in *my* operating room, I would not lose control of my emotions or lash out at colleagues. I also vowed to myself that day that I would never *throw* anything in anger—whether it be scalpels or insults.

Today, more than seven decades later, I find myself wondering if the contaminated scalpel that landed in my arm was any more toxic than the venomous contention that today infects our civic dialogue and too many personal relationships. In this era of polarization and passionate disagreements, rational civility and decency seem to have disappeared in far too many forums.

Vulgarity, faultfinding, judging, and evil speaking of others are all too common.

Too many pundits, politicians, "experts," entertainers, and other influencers seem to throw insults constantly—often to win converts to their point of view and amass a following.

How horrifying it is that so many people act as though it is completely acceptable to condemn, malign, and vilify *anyone* who does not agree with them.

The relentless efforts of cancel culture to render another person unworthy of respect, just because they have a different point of view, are unfair, distressing, and paralyze rich dialogue that could advance a society. Too many individuals of stature seem to feel justified in condemning those who see the world differently than they do.

Many across society seem almost eager to damage another's reputation with pathetic and pithy barbs!

Anger never persuades. Hostility builds no one. Prolonged arguments make enemies out of people who otherwise could become friends. Attacks on other people or points of view invite rebuttals and retribution.

Contention never leads to inspired solutions.

Contentious Behavior Should Not Be the Norm

Regrettably, there is contentious behavior in far too many homes, neighborhoods, and communities. We hear of husbands and wives who belittle each other and their children, of individuals who use angry outbursts to control others, and of those who punish with the "silent treatment." There are employees who defame their colleagues and youth who bully.

And what would we expect? Our teenagers and young adult men and women are only following in the footsteps of their parents, their leaders, and horrific examples portrayed by the media. Tragically, there is a dearth of men and women who model dignified behavior when interacting with those who hold differing opinions.

Dear friends, this should not be. We need to reach out, build bridges of understanding, and seek to learn from one another. Through the years, I have made many friends from diverse political, cultural, and religious backgrounds. I have learned so much from each of them! When it comes to the religions of the world, I cannot identify a single one that does not espouse caring for one another and treating others with the highest respect.

The Lord Jesus Christ left no doubt about how His disciples should treat each other—*especially* when we have differences of opinion. One of the easiest ways to identify a true follower of Jesus Christ is by how compassionately that person treats others.

The Savior made this clear in His Sermon on the Mount and His sermon at the temple in the land Bountiful. "Blessed are the peacemakers," He said.[1] "Agree with thine adversary quickly."[2] "Whosoever shall smite thee on thy right cheek, turn to him the other also."[3] And then, of course, He gave the admonition that challenges each one of us: "Love your enemies, bless them that curse you, do good to them that hate you, and pray for them which despitefully use you, and persecute you."[4]

Before His death, the Savior commanded His Twelve Apostles to love one another as He had loved them.[5] Then He added, "By this shall all men know that ye are my disciples, if ye have love one to another."[6]

These teachings of Jesus Christ make for a great Sunday School lesson, but they can be difficult to put into practice—particularly in today's polarized climate. Admittedly, it is not easy to love those who see the world differently and who advocate for positions different than yours.

And yet, the Savior's message is clear: He admonished His disciples to build, lift, encourage, persuade, and inspire—no matter how difficult the situation. True disciples of Jesus Christ are to be peacemakers. And in my experience, true followers of any of the world's major religions are taught and encouraged likewise.

How We Treat Each Other Matters

One of the best ways we can change this world, and certainly one of the best ways we can honor our Savior, is to become a peacemaker. The Savior's Atonement made it possible for us to overcome *all* evil—including contention.

Make no mistake about it: *contention is evil.* Jesus Christ declared that those who have "the spirit of contention" are not of Him but are "of the devil, who is the father of contention, and [the devil] stirreth up the hearts of men to contend with anger, one with another."[7] Those who foster contention are taking a page out of Satan's playbook, whether they realize it or not. "No man can serve two masters."[8] We cannot support Satan with our verbal assaults and then think that we can still serve God.

How we treat each other matters! How we speak to and about others at home, at work, in the marketplace, at church, and throughout social media matters. How we interact with our family members matters! How we discuss sensitive issues matters! We can literally change our world by interacting with others in a more respectful, dignified way.

I am asking us to interact with others in a higher, holier way. "If there is anything virtuous, lovely, or of good report or praiseworthy"[9] that we can say about another person—whether to his face or behind her back—that should be *our* standard of communication.

If a couple you know gets divorced, or a young missionary returns home early, or a friend doubts her testimony, or a young man says he is gay, none need your judgment. They need to experience the pure love of Jesus Christ reflected in your words and actions.

If a family member rants about her political feelings at your next family gathering, getting on a soapbox will not help anyone. If a friend on social media has strong views that violate *everything* you believe, an angry, cutting retort will not help. To be sure, building bridges of understanding will require much more of you. But that is exactly what your colleague needs. That is what a peacemaker would do.

Be a Model of Peacemaking

Contention drives away the Spirit—every time. It extinguishes feelings of good will and reinforces the false notion that confrontation *is* the way to resolve differences. But it never is.

Contention is a choice. Peacemaking is a choice. We each have our agency to choose contention and separation or to choose peace and reconciliation. I urge you to *choose* to be a peacemaker, now and always.[10]

I repeat that we can literally change the world—one person and one interaction at a time—as we model how honest differences of opinion can be managed with mutual respect and dignified dialogue.

Differences of opinion are part of life. I work every day with dedicated servants of the Lord who do not always see an issue the same way. They know I want to hear their ideas and honest feelings about everything we discuss—*especially* sensitive issues.

My two noble counselors, President Dallin H. Oaks and President Henry B. Eyring, are exemplary in the way they express their feelings—especially when they differ. These are two bright, accomplished men. President Oaks was a distinguished professor at the University of Chicago Law School prior to serving as the president of Brigham Young University and as a justice on Utah's Supreme Court. President Eyring was a professor of business at both the Harvard and Stanford business schools and served as the president of Ricks College (now BYU–Idaho) in Rexburg, Idaho. And yet, these two talented, educated men do not let their intellect or experience get in the way of counseling together in an inspired way.

President Oaks and President Eyring resist the traps we see too often in our society—pride, jealousy, and a thirst for acclaim. Neither demonstrates the pride that suggests he knows better than anyone else and therefore must rigorously defend his position. Neither evidences any jealousy or the need to compete with the other. Because each is filled with charity, "the pure love of Christ,"[11] our deliberations in the First Presidency are guided by the Spirit of the Lord. It is a privilege to work with such brilliant, principled men. How I love them!

In 2018 I met for the first time the leaders of the NAACP (National Association for the Advancement of Colored People). These included NAACP President Derrick Johnson and the Reverend Amos C. Brown, the pastor of the storied 3rd Baptist Church in San Francisco.

As we considered ways to collaborate to improve self-reliance for minority families, we quickly felt deep respect for one another. I was greatly complimented when I was invited to deliver a keynote address at the NAACP National Convention in Detroit in 2019. Reverend Brown introduced me to the NAACP audience as a "brother from another mother." Our common bond as religious believers gave us a natural foundation from which to build a friendship.

Our respective organizations have connected in a significant way. Not as Black or white, not as Baptists or members of the NAACP or The Church of Jesus Christ of Latter-day Saints, but as brothers and sisters working to improve the lives of God's children.

We have learned that we have far more in common than what might divide us. Both of our organizations have learned lessons from the past. It is a joy to listen to each other, consider each other's points of view, and learn together.

Charity Is the Antidote to Contention

Charity is the spiritual gift that helps us to cast off the natural man, who is selfish, defensive, prideful, and jealous. As such, charity—or the pure love of Christ—is the antidote to contention. Charity is the principal characteristic of a true follower of Jesus Christ.[12] Charity defines a peacemaker.

Moroni recorded his father Mormon's words about charity, including his teachings about how to acquire this sublime gift: "Pray unto the Father with all the energy of heart, that ye may be filled with this love, which [our Heavenly Father] hath bestowed upon all who are true followers of his Son, Jesus Christ."[13]

Those blessed with this supernal gift are long-suffering and kind. They do not envy others and are not caught up in their own importance. They are not easily provoked and do not think evil of others. They rejoice in the truth rather than in iniquity.[14]

The pure love of Christ is the answer to the contention that ails the world today. Charity propels us "to bear one another's burdens"[15] rather than heap burdens upon each other. The pure love of Christ allows us to "stand as witnesses of God at all times and in all things"[16]—especially in tense situations when the natural man would be tempted to lash out, criticize, or condemn. Charity allows us to demonstrate how men and women of Christ speak and act—especially when under fire.

The First Presidency receives ambassadors and other dignitaries nearly every week. Our global visitors who seek an appointment represent many faiths, cultures, countries, and races. In these meetings we often discuss complicated issues that do not have simple answers. However, in each meeting we seek to learn from our guests and share meaningful perspectives. Such enriching interactions are possible because we have a sincere desire to build bridges of understanding, and to do so with respect for all.

Acting with Charity Creates a Virtuous Cycle

Now, I am not suggesting "peace at any price." Being a peacemaker does not require us to agree with everyone. But as I have said many times: We can disagree without being disagreeable. Prejudice and bigotry are an affront to all of us. And abuse of any kind—verbal, emotional, physical, or sexual—is intolerable and offends both the laws of God and the laws of man. Charity does not require us to condone the harmful acts of others. Abuse is not to be tolerated under any circumstances.

What I *am* advocating is that we treat others in ways that are consistent with keeping the covenant we make when we partake of the sacrament. We covenant to *always* remember the Savior. Therefore, in situations that are highly charged and filled with contention, I invite you to remember Jesus Christ—in the very moment. Pray to have the courage and wisdom to say or do what He would. As we follow the Prince of Peace, we will become His peacemakers.

Peacemakers Can Help Gather Israel

If you are serious about helping to gather Israel and about building relationships that will last throughout the eternities, *now* is the time to lay aside bitterness. *Now* is the time to cease insisting that it is your way or no way. *Now* is the time to stop doing things that make others walk on eggshells for fear of upsetting you. *Now* is the time to bury your weapons of war.[17] If your verbal arsenal is filled with insults and accusations, now is the time to put them away.[18] As you do so, you will arise as a much stronger man or woman of Christ.

The temple can help us in our quest. There we are endowed with God's power, giving us the ability to overcome Satan, the instigator of *all* contention.[19] Cast him out of your relationships! Please note that we also rebuke the adversary every time we heal a misunderstanding or refuse to take offense. Peacemakers thwart the adversary.

Let us as a people become a true light on the hill—a light that "cannot be hid."[20] Let us show that there is a peaceful, respectful way to resolve complex issues and an enlightened way to work out disagreements. As you demonstrate the charity that true followers of Jesus Christ manifest, the Lord will magnify your efforts beyond your loftiest imagination.

The gospel net is the largest net in the world. God has invited *all* to come unto Him, "black and white, bond and free, male and female."[21] There is room for everyone. However, there is *no* room for prejudice, condemnation, or contention of any kind.

The best is yet to come for those who spend their lives building up others. I invite you to examine your discipleship within the context of the way you treat others. I bless you to make any adjustments that may be needed so that your behavior is ennobling, respectful, and representative of a true follower of Jesus Christ. I bless you to replace belligerence with beseeching, animosity with understanding, and contention with peace.

CHAPTER 6

TREASURE YOUR FAMILY

Nothing produces the joy that families can.

I have lost two daughters to cancer. First to depart was Emily, mother of five, whose final words were: "Don't worry about me, Daddy. I will be all right." The second to leave us was Wendy, mother of seven. In our final interview, I thanked her for being such a righteous daughter and marvelous mother. She mustered a smile and whispered, "Thank you, Daddy."

These were tender, tearful moments. We had worked together, sung together, and often skied together. In both of their final hours, we spoke about things that matter most—faith, covenants, family, love, and eternal life.

I greatly miss our family members who have passed. However, because of the restored gospel of Jesus Christ, I do not worry about them. Because of the restored gospel of Jesus Christ, and the restoration of the priesthood, we have been sealed as a family.

The Savior Himself made it abundantly clear that while His

Resurrection assures that every person who ever lived will indeed be resurrected and live forever,[1] much more is required if we want to have the high privilege of exaltation. Salvation is an individual matter, but exaltation is a family matter.[2]

So, what is required for a family to be exalted forever? We qualify for that privilege by making covenants with God, keeping those covenants, and receiving essential ordinances.

The scriptures are clear about the distinction between a hopeful wish and eternal truth: "All covenants, contracts, . . . obligations, oaths, vows, . . . or expectations, that are *not* made and entered into and sealed by the Holy Spirit of promise, of him who is anointed, both as well for time and for all eternity, . . . are of *no* efficacy, virtue, or force in and after the resurrection from the dead; for all contracts that are not made unto this end have an end when men are dead."[3]

The anguish of my heart is that many people whom I love and respect decline the invitation of Jesus Christ when He says, "Come, follow me."[4]

I understand why God sometimes weeps.[5] I also weep for such friends and relatives. They are wonderful men and women, devoted to their family and civic responsibilities, who give generously of themselves and their resources. The world is better for their efforts. But they have not received the ordinances that will exalt them with their families and bind them together forever.[6]

While there is a place for them hereafter—with other wonderful men and women who also chose not to make or keep covenants with God—it is not the place where families will be reunited and have the privilege to live and progress forever. It is not the kingdom where they will experience the fullness of joy—of never-ending progression and happiness.[7]

I feel to say to my friends who are reticent to make covenants with God: "In this life you never settled for second best in anything.

Yet, as you choose not to make covenants with God, you are settling for a meager roof over your head throughout all eternity. If you truly love your family and if you desire to be with them throughout all eternity, pay the price now—through serious study and fervent prayer—to know these eternal truths and then to abide by them."

Only men and women who are married in the house of the Lord and whose marriage is sealed by the Holy Spirit of Promise will continue as spouses after death and receive the highest degree of celestial glory, or exaltation.[8]

Thus, as grand as the Creation of the earth was, it is only part of something even more magnificent. The earth was created that families might be. For a husband and wife "shall be one flesh, and all this that the earth might answer the end of its creation."[9]

The only thing that satisfies the yearnings of the human spirit is the perpetuation of family love.

Family Life

Family has meant everything to me. My greatest joys and, yes, deepest worries and sorrows, have come from my family. My late wife, Dantzel, and I were blessed with nine daughters and then, finally, a son. Our home was basically a girls' dormitory until Russ Jr. came along! Our daughters showered him with so much love that I'm not sure he knew who his actual mother was for the first several years.

I loved watching our children grow and took pride in their accomplishments. I have welcomed grandchildren and great-grandchildren and now even a great-great-grandson into the world. I have relished every minute we have together in what has become a very large group of people who love being together.

I taught my children to ride bicycles, ski on both snow and water, and drive a car. During the twenty-plus years that we had only daughters in the family, I taught my girls how to mow the lawn and shovel the snow. When Russ Jr. started asking questions about the heart, I took him to the hospital and showed him how to read an angiogram. During the years that Dantzel sang with the Tabernacle Choir, I learned to do the girls' hair on Sunday mornings.

When my schedule at the hospital was particularly intense, Dantzel would load the kids into the station wagon and bring them to the hospital to have dinner with me. I still remember hearing one of my daughters tell a friend that it was "so cool to eat hospital food with Daddy"! Dantzel was the fountain from whom the nourishing love in our family flowed. I worked hard to spend time with our children, but she was the glue that held us together.

My love for my family members is *deep* and *unwavering*. With the miracle of each new baby, more love comes into the family. A newborn baby is completely helpless. When a colt or calf or elephant is born, each can walk on feeble legs. But an infant cannot do much except cry. That dependency upon father and mother requires a husband and wife to work together to serve their baby. This galvanizes their love for each other and their newborn. Family is simply one of the supreme blessings of life!

The sorrows that accompany family life are also very real. In addition to losing two daughters to cancer, I have seen two daughters suffer through divorce. But I have also been grateful for the fine men they later married, once again completing our family circle.

After fifty-nine years of marriage, Dantzel died of a sudden rhythm shift of her heart. Ironically, I had done extensive research on the very malady that claimed her life, yet I could not resuscitate her. I have experienced a widower's silent loneliness.

I also know what it is to be blessed to marry a second time, also to a woman of compassion, intelligence, and generosity of spirit. Wendy has enriched my life beyond measure and filled it with joy.

Nothing compares with the happy companionship between a husband and wife. And nothing provides the joy and growth that come from happy children, grandchildren, and great-grandchildren who make a family circle rich, interesting, and challenging. Among the titles I cherish most are husband, father, and grandfather.

Celestial Marriage

A temple marriage is the marriage our Creator offers His children. All others are man-made. Surely the noblest yearning of the human heart is for a marriage filled with love that endures beyond death. Fidelity to a temple marriage does exactly that. A marriage sealed in the house of the Lord, by the Holy Spirit of Promise, allows families to be together forever.

The Church of Jesus Christ was restored so that families could be sealed and exalted eternally. Celestial marriage brings greater possibilities for happiness than does any other relationship. Marriage is the foundry for social order and the foundation for eternal exaltation. Whenever the scriptures warn that the "earth would be utterly wasted," the warning is connected to the need for priesthood authority to seal families together in holy temples.[10]

The scriptures declare that "it is lawful that [a man] should have one wife, and they twain shall be one flesh, and all this that the earth might answer the end of its creation."[11] Another affirms that "the man [is not] without the woman, neither the woman without the man, in the Lord."[12] Thus, marriage is not only an exalting principle of the gospel; it is a divine commandment. Because a temple marriage is not only between husband and wife but also embraces a partnership with God,[13] when a family is sealed in the temple, that family may become as eternal as the kingdom of God itself.[14]

Mercifully, God's plan of happiness and its exalting blessings can be extended to those who did not have the opportunity to accept the gospel in mortality. This is why proxy temple ordinances are so vital.

Meanwhile, mortal misunderstandings can make mischief in a marriage. In fact, each marriage begins with two built-in handicaps: two imperfect people. This means that happiness in marriage takes real effort from both husband and wife.

When Wendy and I married, we both knew the Lord had orchestrated our relationship. This truth did not, however, mean that our transition was easy at first. I had been married to Dantzel for decades. Wendy was a fifty-five-year-old, never-married woman. We both had expectations for marriage, and those expectations did not entirely match at first. I say this only to suggest that every marriage requires effort, sacrifice, and a steady outpouring of compassion and love.

These many years later, I cannot fathom my life without Wendy, and I feel confident she would say the same. We treasure every moment we have together. So, if you presently have expectations that differ from those of your spouse, keep loving, serving, repenting, forgiving, working, playing, and praying together. The resulting joy will be a marriage that is truly not of this world.

Celestial marriage is a pivotal part of preparation for eternal life. It requires one to be married to the right person, in the right place, by the right authority, and to obey that sacred covenant faithfully.

The Eight "Ates"

The importance of the positive influence of a husband and wife on each other cannot be overstated. I recall a couple I'll refer to as Carla and Carl whom I interviewed about the possibility of presiding over a mission in a distant land. As I described this opportunity to them, Carla sensed Carl's uncertainty. Suddenly she said, "Carl, you can do whatever they ask of you." Then she said to me, "My husband is a righteous man. He knows how to receive revelation. The Lord will help him, and I will stand beside him 100 percent. He can do it!"

Carl subsequently presided over a very challenging mission, and both he and his wife left lasting impressions on the people there. A husband and wife working synergistically together can do infinitely more than either of them can do alone.

May I suggest eight "ates" that can help husbands and wives build strong, lasting relationships:

First, *anticipate.* Think of each other's hopes and needs, and anticipate them.

Second, *appreciate.* Simple expressions of thanks make all the difference. The Lord loves a grateful heart, and so does your companion.

Third, *celebrate.* Don't just remember your wedding anniversary and each other's birthdays, *celebrate them*! Celebrate finding each other! Celebrate your sealing by attending the temple regularly together. Celebrate your love for each other with date nights so that you have time together alone.

Fourth, *cooperate.* Lift each other's load and lighten each other's burdens. Turn to each other first.

Fifth, *elevate.* Do all you can to elevate each other's mood at the end of a long day, or during a difficult challenge, or while sorting through a difference of opinions. Transform problems into opportunities.

Sixth, *motivate.* Encourage your spouse to develop his or her talents, to grow, and to serve. Be the reason your spouse is able to do something he or she might not have thought possible.

Seventh, *radiate.* Try to radiate more light than heat! Work together to make your home a lighthouse for your neighborhood.

Eighth, *supplicate.* When Adam and Eve were cast out of the garden, they "called upon the name of the Lord, and they heard the voice of the Lord . . . speaking unto *them*."[15] Study the gospel together. Grow in spiritual symmetry. Let your home be a house of prayer, a house of faith, and a house of God.[16] Make your home the primary sanctuary of your family's faith. Doing so will bless your marriage in ways you cannot imagine.

The Joy—and Challenge—of Children

I came home from work one evening to find my wife exhausted from a day with nine children underfoot. I offered to get the children ready for bed, but I had also had a long day at the hospital and was trying to get this "chore" done quickly. I began giving orders to our four-year-old daughter: Take your clothes off, put them away, put your pajamas on, brush your teeth, say your prayers. I probably sounded like a drill sergeant. That is when our daughter cocked her head to one side, looked at me with her big, brown eyes, and asked, "Daddy, do you *own* me?"

That question from our precocious preschooler pricked my conscience. "No," I thought to myself, "I do not own my children." Ruling children by command is Satan's technique, not the Savior's.

Children are indeed "an heritage of the Lord,"[17] and we have been commanded to raise them in light and truth.[18] However, no parent is perfect at this. Parenting is arguably the toughest—and most important—job on earth. As parents, we get tired, lose our patience, struggle to understand what our children need, and get worn down by dealing with the same problems again and again. However, we can try our best, and then try again. To weary parents, I say, just keep going, and pray for strength and wisdom to shepherd your children with love. The eventual rewards will be immeasurable.

The Family Is an Incubator of Values

One Saturday afternoon many years ago, I was working in the yard when I heard the bells of the ice cream truck a few houses away. One of my young daughters came running to me and asked for a dime. Sensing the opportunity to teach her an important lesson, I said, "All right, sweetheart, but why don't you work for your money, the same as everyone else does?" Tears instantly began to flow. "But, Daddy," she said, "I don't *like* to work!"

Learning to work is just one of the virtues best modeled and taught in the family. Nowhere are values and virtues taught more persuasively than at home. How blessed are children whose parents model and require high standards of behavior!

As our children were growing up, Dantzel and I found it necessary to establish family standards that our daughters and son did not always appreciate. We established rules to keep them safe, help them make good choices and avoid life-altering mistakes, and encourage their growth.

Our one and only motive for family rules was love. We loved our children so much that we were willing to guide them, protect them, and, yes, sometimes discipline them. Fortunate are the children whose parents say, "Our family behaves this way, *no matter* what those around us are doing!"

The family is the best incubator of virtue, or moral excellence, which encompasses everything from civility to honesty. The virtues of integrity and moral purity are especially important to teach and to live if we care at all about the strength and the joy of our marriage and family.

Integrity is the first rung on the character ladder. Where there is integrity, other virtues follow. Moral transgressions almost always involve some kind of deception. Trust is the keystone that holds every organization together—*especially* marriages and families. Adultery is referred to as "cheating" because it constitutes such a cruel breach of trust. If a man or woman cannot be trusted to honor one of the most sacred commitments they will ever make, who and what will they honor? The Roman statesman Cicero said it this way: "Nothing is more noble, more venerable than fidelity."[19]

My wife Wendy was a professor of marriage and family therapy and a marital therapist *par excellence* for more than thirty years prior to our marriage. I've asked her what percentage of those seeking her help were dealing with some kind of sexual immorality. Her answer? Ninety percent.

Admittedly, moral virtue is fading in the world today. However, it can be a pivotal reality in our lives. President Gordon B. Hinckley declared that "we cannot hope to influence others in the direction of moral virtue unless we live lives of virtue. The example of our virtuous living will carry a greater influence than will all the preaching, postulating, and theorizing in which we might indulge. We cannot expect to lift others unless we are standing on higher ground."[20]

If all of this sounds like beautiful philosophy rather than practical reality, may I encourage you to never underestimate the influence of devoted parents. During my surgical career, I was called to the home of a woman who was in an iron lung. She was so dependent upon this respirator that she could only stay out of it for a minute or two at a time.

During my time in her home, I was fascinated to witness the way her three children interacted with her. One came and said, "Mommy, may I go over to Mary's house to play?" Then a second child came to her side and said, "Mom, will you help me with my math?" Then a third child who was too small to look directly at her mother's face caught her eye through an overhead mirror. She said, "Mother, may I have a cookie?" I choked back tears as I witnessed how strong this mother's influence on her children was, despite the constraints imposed by her weak physical body. It was one of the most impressive parenting moments I have ever seen.

Home-Centered Gospel Teaching

For many years, we in the presiding councils of the Church wrestled with a fundamental dilemma: We realized that as a people, we had become accustomed to thinking of "church" as something that happens in our meetinghouses, supported by what happens at home. We knew we needed an adjustment to this pattern.

In the October 2018 general conference, I announced that it was time for a home-centered Church, supported by what takes place inside our meetinghouses. The long-standing objective of the Church is to assist all members to increase their faith in Jesus Christ and in His Atonement, to assist them in making and keeping their covenants with God, and to strengthen and seal their families. The best place to incubate these spiritual goals and values is at home.

I began to appreciate this reality when my older daughters were teenagers. One day I had the distinct impression that my girls were asking me "branch and leaf" gospel questions and I was giving them "branch and leaf" answers. I needed to help them get to the root of what we believe. I only wish I had had the *Come, Follow Me* program to assist me in those days. It is designed to do exactly what I attempted to do on my own so many years ago.

What can you teach your children to help them get to the root of the gospel and firmly secure their own testimonies?

Above all, teach them to know and love God their Heavenly Father. Help them to know that they are created in His image. Each son or daughter is a spirit child of God with a divine nature. Help your children learn to pray to their Heavenly Father, morning and night.

Teach your children to love the Lord Jesus Christ. Teach them about the Lord's Atonement, which enables them to repent and to do things they will never be able to do on their own.

Teach your children about prophets, with an important emphasis on the Prophet Joseph Smith and the living prophets.

Help your children understand the significance of the Book of Mormon as Another Testament of Jesus Christ and an important anchor to their testimony. Allow them to hear their father's and mother's voice reading to them, and have them read to you. Home is the best place to establish a pattern of scripture study.

Teach your children to love the temple and to live worthily so they can participate in proxy baptisms as teenagers, be endowed as an adult, and be married there. Display a picture of the temple in each child's bedroom.

Teach your children to pay tithing, to obey the Word of Wisdom, and to prepare to serve a mission. Encourage them to get as much education as they can and to be good citizens of the nation in which they live.

Now, this may seem like an impossible list of things to teach and model. But over time, natural opportunities will present themselves to underscore these fundamental truths.

Be willing to discuss questions that your children have about Church doctrine, policies, and procedures. If they express doubts, talk with them openly about their concerns. Don't hesitate to admit when you don't know the answers, and invite your children to join you in seeking answers from trustworthy sources such as the scriptures and general conference talks.

Do all you can to make your home the incubator for your

children's gospel knowledge and the center of his or her personal gospel study.

The Impact of Strong Families

I recall the day I saw a young boy who was about twelve years old wearing a T-shirt with big bold letters that declared, "I AM the future!" How right he was! The family is the seedbed of future generations.

When families are strong, societies are strong. When families are weak and riddled with problems, societies ultimately falter and collapse under the weight of social needs too massive for any government to meet. This is not opinion; it is fact borne out not only by one civilization after another but by volumes of research gathered in our day—all of which demonstrates that children from intact families are happier, healthier, and more likely to become productive adults. As two seasoned scholars have indicated, "Disease, depression, and early death come to those who reject family life. This result should not really cause surprise. Science, after all, is the study of the natural order. And while the Creator forgives, nature never does."[21]

Some years ago, the *Ladies' Home Journal* published an article from a journalist who had traveled to China with her husband. She found herself taking pictures of women with their children rather than of famous landmarks. "After I returned home and had the pictures developed," she wrote, "I kept looking at them. Especially at the children. They were so utterly sweet, so utterly small. I felt a pain in my chest; I was as sad and bereft as I have ever been in my life. It was at that moment I began grieving that I had never had children of my own."[22]

As declared in the Proclamation on the Family, "The family is ordained of God. Marriage between man and woman is essential to

His eternal plan. Children are entitled to birth within the bonds of matrimony, and to be reared by a father and a mother who honor marital vows with complete fidelity."

These profound, declarative sentences contain the secret to happiness in this life and outline the gateway to eternal life.

CHAPTER 7

RESPECT THE SPIRITUAL STRENGTH OF WOMEN

Women of faith are our hope for the future.

Throughout my life, I have been surrounded by remarkable women—beginning with my dear mother. No boy ever had a more supportive, devoted mother. Though she never said it expressly, she let me know, by the way she treated me, that she trusted me to make good decisions.

Then, as a young man, how fortunate I was to marry my first wife, Dantzel. Her testimony and devotion to the gospel strengthened my testimony. She was the heart of our home and an anchor for our children. During my years of heavy professional responsibilities, she was the rudder that kept our family headed in the right direction. She infused joy into our home and was a mother without peer.

I scarcely know where to begin to articulate the strengths of our nine daughters. They have brought nonstop joy to this daddy's heart. Watching them grow up and emulate the strengths of their mother has been a sheer delight. I see Dantzel in each one of them! They are generous, compassionate, and loving. But they also have backbones of steel. They are firm in their faith, eager to learn and experience new things, and unflappable. They get all of that from their mother.

When Dantzel passed away, I was bereft. I could not imagine ever filling the void in my heart or in my life. But in the Lord's mercy, He presented me with the opportunity to marry again, to another astonishingly strong and wise woman—my wife Wendy. She has transformed my life in ways that would be difficult to describe. Her insights about people and human nature are second to none. Her faith is unwavering. When she agreed to marry me, literally everything about her life changed. Through the years we have been together, she has not only blessed me but the entire Church.

In addition to these close familial relationships, I have served alongside countless sisters in the Church who have been called to positions of leadership. Again and again, I have witnessed their spiritual strength, ability to receive revelation, and pure determination to stand for truth and righteousness. Sister leaders throughout the Church bless the kingdom of God in irreplaceable ways. Those with whom I have served have, on many occasions, opened my eyes to new insights.

Throughout my life I have been amazed at the influence women have on the rising generations. I resonate with a statement Elder Neal A. Maxwell made: "When the real history of mankind is fully disclosed, will it feature the echoes of gunfire or the shaping sound of lullabies? . . . Will what happened in cradles and kitchens prove to be more controlling than what happened in congresses? When the surf of the centuries has made the great pyramids so much sand, the everlasting family will still be standing, because it is a celestial institution, formed outside telestial time. The women of God know this."[1]

I reverence the unique strengths and capacities of women. In fact, one day while I was speaking to a congregation in South America, I became quite excited about my message and at a pivotal moment I said—complete with animated hand movements—"As the *mother* of ten children, I can tell you that . . ." and then I went on to complete that sentence.

I did not realize that I had said the word *mother*. My translator assumed I had misspoken and changed the word to *father*, so the congregation never knew I had referred to myself as a *mother*. But Wendy heard it, and she was delighted with my Freudian slip.

I think in that moment, my deep longing to make a difference in the world—like only a mother does—bubbled up from my heart. Through the years, whenever I have been asked why I chose to become a medical doctor, I have responded, "Because I could not *choose* to be a mother."

Now, let's be clear about an important doctrinal understanding. When I speak about "mothers," I am not referring solely to those who have given birth or adopted children in this life. I am including *all* of our Heavenly Father's adult daughters. *Every* woman is a mother by virtue of her eternal identity and divine destiny. Eve was designated as the "mother of all living"[2] before she ever bore a child on this earth.

No one can duplicate the influence of a mother, however or wherever that mothering influence is expressed. Men can, and often do, communicate the love of Heavenly Father and the Savior to others. But women have a special gift for doing so—a divine endowment. Sisters have the innate capacity and gift to sense what someone needs—and *when* he or she needs it. Women seem to instinctively know how to reach out, comfort, teach, and strengthen someone in his or her moment of need.

It was our glorious Mother Eve—with her far-reaching vision of our Heavenly Father's plan—who initiated the Fall. Her wise and courageous choice, with Adam's supporting decision, moved forward God's plan of happiness. Their choice made it possible for each of us to come to earth, receive a body, and prove that we would choose to stand up for Jesus Christ here, just as we did in the premortal world.

I urge all women to pray to understand their unique spiritual gifts and to cultivate, use, and expand them even more than they have before. Women will literally change the world as they do so. In fact, *I have no reservation in declaring that women—and especially women of faith—are our hope for the future!*

Faithful Women Are Unusual Exemplars

The spring and early summer of 2015 proved to be momentous for the Church as well as for me personally. President Boyd K. Packer and Elder L. Tom Perry, both senior to me in the Quorum of the Twelve Apostles, died within thirty-four days of each other.[3] I had served with and learned from these Brethren since my call to the Twelve more than thirty years earlier. For them both suddenly to be gone was a shock to my spiritual system. They were treasured friends and magnificent servants of the Lord. With little warning, I became the President of the Quorum of the Twelve Apostles.

I was with both President Packer and Elder Perry during their final days, and one of the impressions that has lingered with me ever since is what I observed in Sister Donna Packer and Sister Barbara Perry. Etched in my mind are the serene images of them at their husbands' bedsides, both women filled with love, truth, and pure faith.

As Sister Packer sat next to her husband in his final hours, she radiated peace. Though she realized that her beloved companion of almost seventy years would soon depart, she showed the tranquility of a woman filled with faith. She seemed absolutely angelic.

I saw the same kind of love and faith emanate from Sister Perry. Her devotion to both her husband and the Lord was obvious, and it moved me deeply.

Through their husbands' final hours, these stalwart women modeled the strength and courage that covenant-keeping women always demonstrate.

It would be impossible to measure the influence that such women have, not only on families but also in the Lord's Church, as wives, mothers, and grandmothers; as sisters, aunts, and friends; as teachers and leaders; and especially as exemplars, mentors, and devout defenders of the faith. So many of our sisters today exemplify the courage of Mother Eve; the radiant faith and purity of Mary, the mother of Jesus; and the kind of influence that Rebekah had on Isaac as well as their son Jacob.[4]

The Women of This Dispensation Are Unique

Women have modeled supreme faith and devotion in every gospel dispensation. Yet the women of this dispensation are distinct from the women of any other because this dispensation is distinct from any other. All previous dispensations were limited to a small segment of the world and were terminated by apostasy. In contrast, this dispensation will not be limited in location or time. It will fill the world and merge with the Second Coming of the Lord.[5] This is the dispensation our forefathers have "awaited with anxious expectation" and is the one in which "nothing shall be withheld"[6] from the Saints.

In 1979, President Spencer W. Kimball made a profound prophecy about the impact that covenant-keeping women would have on the future of the Lord's Church. Said he: "Much of the major growth that is coming to the Church in the last days will come because many of the good women of the world . . . will be drawn to the Church in large numbers. This will happen to the degree that the women of the Church reflect righteousness and articulateness in their lives and to the degree that the women of the Church are seen as distinct and different—in happy ways—from the women of the world."[7]

I have no hesitation in declaring that the day that President Kimball foresaw is *today*. The righteous women of the Lord's Church *today* are the ones President Kimball foresaw! Their virtue, light, love, knowledge, courage, character, and faith will draw good women of the world, along with their families, to the Church in unprecedented numbers.

The Church needs the strength, conversion, conviction, ability to lead, wisdom, and articulate voices of devoted, principled women of faith. The kingdom of God cannot be complete without women who make sacred covenants and then keep them—women who can speak with the power and authority of God!

President Joseph Fielding Smith told the sisters of Relief Society, "You can speak with authority, because the Lord has placed authority upon you." He also said that the Relief Society has "been given power and authority to do a great many things. The work which they do is done by divine authority."[8]

We need women who know how to make important things happen by their faith and who are courageous defenders of morality and families in a sin-sick world. We need women who are devoted to shepherding God's children along the covenant path toward exaltation; women who know how to receive personal revelation, who understand the power and peace of the temple endowment; women who know how to call upon the powers of heaven to protect and strengthen children and families.

Dantzel was such a woman. I will always be grateful for the life-changing influence she had on me in all aspects of my life, including my pioneering efforts in open-heart surgery.

Many years ago, I was asked to operate on a little girl, gravely ill from congenital heart disease. Her older brother had died of a similar condition. Her parents pleaded for help. I was not optimistic about the outcome but vowed to do all in my power to save her life. Despite my best efforts, the child died. Later, the same parents brought another daughter to me, then just sixteen months old. She, too, was born with a malformed heart. Again, at their request, I performed an operation. This child also died. This third heartbreaking loss in one family devastated me.

I went home grief-stricken. I threw myself upon our living room floor and cried all night long. Dantzel stayed by my side, listening as I repeatedly declared that I would never perform another heart operation. Then, around 5:00 in the morning, she looked at me and said, "Are you finished crying? Then get dressed. Go back to the lab. Go to work. You need to learn more. If you quit now, others will have to painfully learn what you already know."

How I needed her vision, love, and determination! I went back to work and learned more. If it were not for Dantzel's inspired prodding, I am not sure that I would have pursued open-heart surgery further. Thus, I would not have been prepared to perform the operation in 1972 that saved the life of President Spencer W. Kimball.[9]

I pray that our sisters realize the breadth and scope of their influence when they courageously speak those things that come to their hearts and minds as directed by the Spirit.

A wise stake president reported about a stake council meeting in which they were wrestling with a difficult challenge. At one point, he realized that the stake Primary president had not spoken, so he asked if she had any impressions. "Well, actually, I do," she said, and then proceeded to share an insight that changed the entire direction of the meeting. The stake president concluded, "As she spoke, the Spirit testified to me that she had given voice to the revelation we had been seeking as a council."

I dearly wish for our sisters, whatever their calling or circumstances, to know that the Church at every level needs their impressions, their insights, and their inspiration. We need them to speak up and speak out in ward and stake councils. We need each married sister to speak as "a *contributing* and *full* partner"[10] as she unites with her husband in governing their family. Married or single, old or young, highly educated or trained by the school of life, our sisters possess distinctive capabilities and special intuition they have received as gifts from God. We brethren cannot duplicate their unique insights and influence.

Women Have Access to Priesthood Power

As innately and divinely talented as women are, they do not need to rely solely upon their own gifts and talents.

I vividly remember walking out of the temple one day with Wendy and saying to her, "I hope the sisters understand the spiritual treasures that are theirs in the temple." I have often found myself thinking about this, including during two visits Wendy and I made to Harmony, Pennsylvania, where both the Aaronic and Melchizedek Priesthoods were restored.

It was in Harmony that Emma Hale Smith served as her husband's first scribe as the Prophet translated the Book of Mormon. It was also in Harmony that Joseph received a revelation manifesting the Lord's will to Emma. The Lord instructed her to expound the scriptures, exhort the Church, receive the Holy Ghost, and spend her time "learning much." Emma was also counseled to "lay aside the things of this world, and seek for the things of a better." The Lord concluded His instruction to her with these compelling words: "This is my voice unto all."[11]

Everything that happened in Harmony, Pennsylvania, has important implications for the life of every covenant daughter of God. How I yearn for each sister in the Church to understand that the restoration of the priesthood is just as relevant to her as a woman as it is to any man. Because the Melchizedek Priesthood has been restored, both covenant-keeping women and men have access to "all the spiritual blessings of the church"[12] or to the spiritual treasures the Lord has for His children.

Every woman and every man who makes covenants with God and keeps those covenants, and who participates worthily in priesthood ordinances, has direct access to the power of God. Those who are endowed in the house of the Lord receive a gift of God's priesthood power by virtue of their covenant, along with a gift of knowledge to know how to draw upon that power.

The heavens are just as open to women who are endowed with God's power flowing from their priesthood covenants as they are to men who bear the priesthood! Women have the right to draw liberally upon the Savior's power to help their families and others they love.

The process for doing so is not spelled out in any manual. However, for all who want to better understand, the Holy Ghost will be your personal tutor. He will teach you what the Lord would have you study, know, and do. The process of learning how to draw upon priesthood power is neither quick nor easy, but it *is* spiritually invigorating. What could possibly be more exciting than laboring with the Spirit to understand God's power—priesthood power?

Accessing the power of God in our lives requires each of us to do the same things that the Lord instructed Emma to do. As each sister in the Church prayerfully studies section 25 of the Doctrine and Covenants, the Holy Ghost will enlighten her mind.

Learning to draw upon priesthood power requires each sister to put aside many things of this world. Sometimes we speak almost casually about walking away from the world with its temptations and false philosophies. But doing so requires us to examine our lives repeatedly. As we do so, the Holy Ghost will prompt us about what is no longer needful or worthy of our time and energy.

A Word of Warning

The adversary does not want women to understand either the covenants they made at baptism or the profound endowment of knowledge and power they have received—or will yet receive—in the house of the Lord. Satan certainly does not want women to understand that every time they worthily serve and worship in the temple, they leave armed with God's power and with His angels having "charge over" them.[13]

Satan and his minions will constantly create roadblocks to prevent women from understanding the spiritual gifts with which they have been and can be blessed. Unfortunately, some roadblocks may be the result of another's misbehavior. It grieves me to think that any woman has been marginalized or abused by a husband, father, or supposed friend, or has not been believed by a priesthood leader. I feel deep sorrow to think that any woman may have felt sidelined, disrespected, or misjudged. Such offenses have no place in the kingdom of God.

Conversely, it thrills me when I learn of priesthood leaders who eagerly seek the participation of women in ward and stake councils. I am inspired by each husband who demonstrates by his words and actions that his most important priesthood responsibility is to care for his wife.[14] I praise that man who deeply respects his wife's ability to receive revelation and treasures her as an equal partner in their marriage. That is how it should be. That is how it needs to be!

Righteous Women Inspire Respect

When a man understands the majesty and power of a righteous, endowed Latter-day Saint woman, is it any wonder that he feels like standing when she enters the room?

From the dawning of time, women have been blessed with a

unique moral compass—the ability to distinguish right from wrong and truth from deception. This gift is enhanced in those who make and keep covenants.

We know that the culminating act of all Creation was the creation of woman! All of the purposes of the world, and all that was in the world, would have been for naught without women, who are a keystone in the priesthood arch of Creation.[15] Or, as President Gordon B. Hinckley explained, Eve was "the grand summation of all of the marvelous work that had gone before."[16]

Attacks against the Church and our way of life as true disciples of Jesus Christ are going to increase. Therefore, we need women who have a bedrock understanding of the doctrine of Christ and who will use that understanding to teach and help to raise a sin-resistant generation.[17] We need women who can detect deception in all of its forms. We need women who know how to access the power of God. We need women who have the courage and vision of our Mother Eve. We need women who teach and model the doctrine of Christ.

The Lord and His Church need women who are fully engaged in helping to gather Israel. Righteous women shape the future! *They are our hope for the future!*

It is truly converted, covenant-keeping women—women like my dear wife Wendy—whose righteous lives will increasingly stand out in a deteriorating world and who will thus be seen as distinct and different in the *happiest* of ways.

Because women of faith are our hope for the future!

CHAPTER 8

RESPECT PRIESTHOOD POWER

Righteous exercise of priesthood authority can change the course of the world.

On September 19, 2015, I participated in what was, to that point in my life, the most significant priesthood assignment I had ever received. President Thomas S. Monson had assigned me to dedicate the renovated Priesthood Restoration Site near Harmony, Pennsylvania. Both the anticipation of that event and the actual experience itself moved me deeply. Other than the Sacred Grove and a few additional landmarks in and around Palmyra, New York, there may be no other location in Church history as central to the Restoration of the gospel of Jesus Christ as is the area in and around Harmony, Pennsylvania.

Wendy and I were joined there by Bishop Gary E. Stevenson, then the Presiding Bishop, and his wife, Lesa, and Elder Steven E. Snow of the Seventy, then the Church Historian and Recorder, with his wife, Phyllis. As we walked along a new trail system installed throughout the woods where both the Aaronic and Melchizedek

Priesthoods were restored, Wendy and I commented to each other that the reality of priesthood keys and priesthood power was tangible. We were walking through sacred maple woods where John the Baptist returned as a resurrected being to confer the Aaronic Priesthood upon Joseph Smith and Oliver Cowdery. This was holy ground. Shortly thereafter, Peter, James, and John, also as resurrected beings, conferred the Melchizedek Priesthood.

In Harmony, Joseph and Emma lived near Emma's parents and enjoyed a spiritual solitude and degree of protection that allowed Joseph to focus on the translation of the Book of Mormon. It was also a time of intense tutoring as the Lord taught Joseph about his divinely appointed role as prophet, seer, and revelator and restored the priesthood through Joseph so that he could preside as the Prophet of this last dispensation. Joseph's time in Harmony proved to be a formative season of translation, revelation, and restoration.[1] Wendy and I were both deeply affected by our experience on those sacred grounds.

The reason for such a profound feeling of reverence is clear. The restoration of priesthood keys to the earth was crucial. Priesthood keys authorize men on earth to act and speak in the name of God.

Priesthood authority is likewise real. Adam received priesthood authority before the world was formed.[2] Very simply, the priesthood "is the consummate power on this earth. It is the power by which the earth was created."[3] The Prophet Joseph Smith added that "the Priesthood is an everlasting principle, and existed with God from eternity, and will to eternity."[4] President Joseph F. Smith described the priesthood as "the power of God delegated to man by which man can act in the earth for the salvation of the human family."[5]

Speaking about the keys of the priesthood, President M. Russell Ballard taught this important truth: "Those who have priesthood keys . . . literally make it possible for all who serve faithfully under their direction to exercise priesthood authority and have access to priesthood power."[6]

Prior to being ordained an Apostle, I held priesthood keys just one time—when I served as president of the Bonneville Utah Stake. While serving as stake president, I experienced the power of those keys to help the members of my stake.

Then, on April 12, 1984, I had the sacred experience of having the First Presidency and members of the Quorum of the Twelve Apostles ordain me an Apostle and confer *all* of the restored keys of the priesthood upon me. From that moment, I began to feel the weight of the responsibility of those keys and the burden of timeless trust that accompanies them. I have experienced the power of those keys again and again as I have traversed the earth. I know without reservation that priesthood keys have been restored to the earth "for the last days and for the last time."[7]

On January 14, 2018, the members of the Quorum of the Twelve and my counselors in the newly reconstituted First Presidency, President Dallin H. Oaks and President Henry B. Eyring, placed their hands on my head. With President Oaks acting as voice, they set me apart as the President of the Church.

One of the things I have learned in my life is how very real priesthood keys, priesthood authority, and priesthood power are. I have also learned that the privileges both men and women receive because of the restoration of the priesthood are tangible and can literally change the lives of all who believe in and learn to draw upon priesthood power.

The Impact of Priesthood Authority

The restoration of the priesthood of God opens to Latter-day Saints the greatest of all spiritual blessings, because the Melchizedek

Priesthood holds "the keys of all the spiritual blessings of the church."[8] These blessings are equally available to women, men, and children.

As I have traveled the earth for virtually forty years as an Apostle, I have met numerous faithful women who understand the power inherent in their callings as well as in their endowment and other temple ordinances. As described in the previous chapter, these women know how to call upon the powers of heaven to protect and strengthen their husbands, children, and others they love. How inspired I am by them!

Likewise, I have met countless faithful men who live up to their privileges as bearers of the priesthood. They bless, guide, heal, and protect others with the priesthood they hold. They shun evil and are mighty elders in Israel. I am inspired by priesthood-bearing men who work tirelessly to strengthen others.

The Joy of Bearing the Priesthood

There is pure joy in bearing the priesthood and in having the capacity and authority to bless and help others.

In the previous chapter, I referred to the family of Ruth and Jimmy Hatfield, and particularly to their two daughters—Laurel Ann and Gay Lynn—who were born with congenital heart defects. I described how heartbroken I was when both girls died following their operations. However, my grief paled in comparison to Ruth's and Jimmy's. Understandably, they were spiritually and emotionally shattered and were furious with me for not being able to save their daughters' lives.

Over time, I learned that the Hatfields harbored lingering resentment toward me and, by extension, the Church. For almost six decades, I was haunted by this situation and grieved for the

Hatfields. I tried several times to establish contact with them, but without success.

Then one night in May 2015, I was awakened by Laurel Ann and Gay Lynn Hatfield, who live on the other side of the veil. Though I did not see or hear them with my physical senses, I felt their presence. Spiritually, I heard their pleadings. Their message was brief and clear: "Brother Nelson, we are not sealed to anyone! Can you help us?" Prompted by this vivid experience, I again sought to make contact with the family. I learned that Ruth Hatfield was deceased but Jimmy was alive and living with his son Shawn.

When I reached out this time to Jimmy Hatfield, he and Shawn agreed to meet with me.

When I met with Jimmy, then eighty-eight, and Shawn, I literally knelt in front of Jimmy and spoke to him from my heart. I told him about his daughters' pleadings and said that I would be honored to perform sealing ordinances for his family. I also explained that it would take time and effort on his and Shawn's part to be ready to enter the temple, as neither of them were endowed.

The Spirit of the Lord was powerful throughout that meeting. When Jimmy and Shawn accepted my offer, I was overjoyed! From that day forward they began to work with their stake president and bishop to prepare for the temple. Home teachers,[9] the ward mission leader, a pair of young missionaries, and a senior missionary couple lent support. After a period of time, I had the privilege of sealing Jimmy to his deceased wife, Ruth, and then their four children to them. Wendy and I wept as we participated in that sublime experience. Many hearts were healed that day!

Since that experience, I have marveled at what Jimmy and Shawn were willing to do. If I could have the wish of my heart, it would be that each man and young man in this Church would demonstrate the courage, strength, and humility of this father and son.

They were willing to forgive and let go of old hurts and habits. They were willing to submit to guidance from their priesthood leaders so that the Atonement of Jesus Christ could purify and magnify them. They were willing to become men who worthily bear the priesthood "after the holiest order of God."[10]

To *bear* means to support the weight of that which is held. It is a sacred trust to bear the priesthood. I am often overwhelmed with the reality that the priesthood conferred upon worthy males is the *very same power and authority* through which God created this and numberless worlds, governs the heaven and the earth, and exalts His obedient children.[11]

Bearing the priesthood of God is one of the greatest privileges God affords His sons here on earth.

Exercising Priesthood Power

I recall an occasion when Wendy and I were in a meeting where the organist was poised and ready to play the opening hymn. When he began pressing the keys, there was no sound. I whispered to Wendy, "He has no power." Something had interrupted the flow of electrical power to the organ.

In like manner, I fear that too many men have been given the *authority* of the priesthood but lack priesthood *power* because the flow of power has been blocked by laziness, dishonesty, pride, immorality, or preoccupation with things of the world. I fear there are too many priesthood bearers who have done very little to develop their ability to call upon priesthood power. I worry about those who have impure thoughts, feelings, or actions, thereby cutting off priesthood power. I fear that too many have surrendered their agency to the adversary and are in essence saying, "I care more about satisfying my own desires than I do about bearing the priesthood of God to bless my family and others."

I fear that some men may one day wake up and realize what power in the priesthood really is. I fear that they will be overwhelmed with deep regret that they spent far more time seeking power *over* others than learning to exercise fully the power of God to bless others. For "the rights of the priesthood are inseparably connected with the powers of heaven," and the "powers of heaven cannot be controlled nor handled only upon the principles of righteousness."[12]

Surely none of us would intentionally choose to waste our days and settle for Esau's mess of pottage[13] when we have been entrusted with the possibility of receiving all of the blessings of Abraham![14]

In a coming day, *only* those men who have respected the priesthood they bear, by *diligently* seeking to be taught by the Lord Himself, will be able to bless, guide, protect, strengthen, and heal others—including their own families. Only a man who has paid the price for priesthood power will be able to bring miracles to those he loves and keep his marriage and family safe, now and throughout eternity.

What Can Priesthood Bearers Do?

Not terribly long ago, I attended a sacrament meeting in which an infant received a name and father's blessing. The young father held his precious daughter in his arm, gave her a name, and then offered a beautiful *prayer*. But he did *not* give his daughter a blessing. That sweet baby girl got a name but no blessing. That elder did not know the difference between a prayer and a priesthood blessing. With his priesthood authority and power, he could have blessed his infant, but he did not. He also failed to acknowledge that he was blessing his daughter in the name of Jesus Christ and by the power of the Holy Melchizedek Priesthood. It was a series of unfortunate missed opportunities.

We perhaps all know of brethren who set apart sisters as Primary, Young Women, and Relief Society leaders and teachers but who fail to bless them with the power to fulfill their callings. They give only instructions.

In this regard, President Dallin H. Oaks made a significant clarification that both men and women need to understand: "We are not accustomed to speaking of women having the authority of the priesthood in their Church callings, but what other authority can it be? When a woman . . . is set apart to preach the gospel as a full-time missionary, she is given priesthood authority to perform a priesthood function. The same is true when a woman is set apart to function as an officer or teacher in a Church organization under the direction of one who holds the keys of the priesthood. Whoever functions in an office or calling received from one who holds priesthood keys exercises priesthood authority in performing her or his assigned duties."[15]

Further examples of missed opportunities are worthy fathers who fail to give their wives and children priesthood blessings when they need them. Far too many of our brothers and sisters go through trials without ever receiving a true priesthood blessing that calls down power from heaven to help them and bless them with peace.

On the other hand, I was deeply grateful to learn of countless priesthood-bearing men who conducted meaningful, Spirit-filled sacrament meetings in their homes during the COVID-19 pandemic, when such was authorized. I am always moved when I learn about priesthood bearers who instantly come to the aid of those who need a priesthood blessing.

To the brethren of the Church, we hold the priesthood of God!

We have His authority to bless His people. Consider the remarkable assurance the Lord gave us when He said, "Whomsoever you bless I will bless."[16] It is our privilege to act in the name of Jesus Christ to bless God's children according to His will for them.

Priesthood Bearers Can Change Lives

Years ago, as a resident surgeon at the Massachusetts General Hospital, I was on duty every day, every other night, and every other weekend. There was not much time left for my wife, our four children, and Church assignments. Nonetheless, our branch president assigned me to visit the home of Wilbur and Leonora Cox. This couple had been sealed in the temple, but Wilbur had not participated in the Church for quite some time.

My companion and I went to their home. As we entered, Sister Cox welcomed us warmly, but Brother Cox walked into another room and closed the door. After a while, I went to the closed door and knocked. When I finally heard a muffled, "Come in," I opened the door to find Brother Cox surrounded by an array of amateur radio equipment. As I entered, he lit up a cigar. Clearly, I was not welcome.

Looking at the radio equipment, I said, "Brother Cox, I have always wanted to learn more about amateur radio work. Would you be willing to teach me about it if I came back at another time?"

He reluctantly agreed, and that proved to be the beginning of a dear friendship. Through many subsequent visits, the greatness of Wilbur Cox emerged. After our family moved away, others continued to nurture the Cox family. In 1954, branch president Ira Terry called Wilbur to be the branch Sunday School superintendent. Wilbur accepted the calling and dropped any habits that violated the Word of Wisdom.

About eight years after that first visit, the Boston Stake was created.[17] Imagine who was its first stake president. Yes! Brother Wilbur Cox! During subsequent years, he also served as a mission president and a temple president.

Years later, as a member of the Quorum of the Twelve, I was assigned to create a new stake in Sanpete County, Utah. During the usual interviews to identify a stake president, I was delighted to encounter again my friend Brother Cox and felt impressed to call him as patriarch of the new stake. After I ordained him, we embraced each other and wept. Others in the room probably wondered why two grown men were crying, but we knew. Ours were tears of joy!

The account does not end there. Brother and Sister Cox's family grew to include three children, twenty grandchildren, and fifty-four great-grandchildren. Add to that their impact on hundreds of missionaries and new members, on thousands more in the temple, and on hundreds more who received patriarchal blessings at the hands of Patriarch Cox. His and Leonora's influence will continue to ripple through many generations to come.

The work of saving souls is real, and priesthood power is what makes it possible. The gathering—on both sides of the veil—changes the course of countless lives. Bearers of the priesthood have vital, irreplaceable roles in this work.

The Price of Bearing the Priesthood

What is the price priesthood bearers must pay to learn to officiate in the offices of the priesthood and draw upon priesthood power? The Savior's senior Apostle, Peter, declared the qualities we should seek to have in order to "be partakers of the divine nature" and escape the corruption of the world.[18]

Peter named faith, virtue, knowledge, temperance, patience,

godliness, brotherly kindness, charity, and diligence.[19] And let us not forget humility![20] None of us is perfect. However, the more we consistently seek to develop these godly attributes, the greater will be our ability to exercise priesthood power.

We can also increase our ability to exercise priesthood power by praying from the depths of our hearts. Routine recitations of past and upcoming activities, punctuated with requests for blessings, does not constitute the kind of communing with God that brings enduring power. Pray *to know how to pray* with power. Enos learned how. After wrestling "before God" for a remission of his sins, he cried unto the Lord "in mighty prayer."[21] Each one of us can do the exact same thing. God will teach anyone who sincerely wants to communicate with Him how to pray.

Diligently and consistently searching the scriptures and learning to literally feast on the words of Christ[22] will increase your access to more power. If you want to melt your wife's heart, let her find you studying the doctrine of Christ.[23] There is no better way to be prepared, at a moment's notice, to give a priesthood blessing and help someone in need than to regularly immerse yourself in the word of God. The Lord will honor your consistent efforts by allowing you to truly speak in His name as you serve and bless others.

Worshipping in the temple regularly will also increase your ability to exercise priesthood power. The temple is a "house of learning"[24] with which the world's finest universities cannot compare. There is no better place to ask the Lord to tutor you about priesthood keys, priesthood authority, and priesthood power.[25] "Ask, and ye shall receive; knock, and it shall be opened unto you."[26]

As you give the same amount of time to gaining priesthood power as you do to your work and recreation, the heavens will open. As you humbly present yourself before the Lord and ask Him to teach you how to better exercise priesthood power, He will show you how. And, as you pay the price, your relationships with your Heavenly Father, Jesus Christ, your wife, children, friends, and associates at work will improve in ways you cannot presently imagine.

Faith in the Oath and Covenant of the Priesthood

If you at times wonder if you have what it takes to meet the obligations that fall to those who are ordained to the priesthood, consider this promise from the Lord: "For whoso is faithful unto the obtaining these two priesthoods of which I have spoken, and the magnifying their calling, are sanctified by the Spirit unto the renewing of their bodies."[27]

I have seen this promise fulfilled time and again in the life of aging prophets who were able to powerfully testify of the Lord Jesus Christ even though their bodies were frail. I have seen bishops, stake presidents, and mission presidents the world over serve until they felt they had nothing left to give—and then serve some more. I am presently experiencing the sustaining strength and renewal by the Lord in my own life as I age. I am grateful to experience how very real the power in the oath and covenant of the priesthood is.[28]

I sustain what President Henry B. Eyring said about those who bear the priesthood of God: "The very fact that you have been offered the oath and covenant is evidence that God has chosen you, knowing your power and capacity. He has known you since you were with Him in the spirit world. With His foreknowledge of your strength, He has allowed you to find the true Church of Jesus Christ and to be offered the priesthood. You can feel confidence because you have evidence of His confidence in you."[29]

Men who worthily bear the priesthood of God have access to and can officiate in the greatest power in heaven or on earth.

This means that, through the grace and power of God, priesthood-bearing men can change the quality and course of endless lives.

Thus, bearers of the priesthood can literally change the course of the world.

PART 3

LAWS FOR ACCOMPLISHING THE IMPOSSIBLE

CHAPTER 9

EXPERIENCE THE HEALING POWER OF GRATITUDE

Life-altering gratitude is not just for good things.

As a man of faith, and also as a man of science, the worldwide COVID-19 pandemic was of great interest to me.

As a man of science, I immediately appreciated the critical need to prevent the spread of infection and disease. It was inspiring to witness the devoted service of healthcare professionals all over the world who worked tirelessly to save lives. During those early days of the pandemic in the spring and summer of 2020, I felt enormous empathy for the doctors and epidemiologists working around the clock to fight a virus they had never seen before.

I know what it's like to grapple for answers to medical dilemmas. It can be unnerving, especially when lives are at stake. Like the rest of the world, I grieved for the millions of individuals whose lives were changed or ended by COVID-19.

As a man of faith, however, I viewed the pandemic somewhat differently. I saw it as only one of many ills that plague our world.

One might argue that hate, civil unrest, racism, violence, dishonesty, vulgarity, anger, and what seems to be an ever-increasing lack of civility are equally corrosive and even deadly not only to society but to our individual hearts and minds.

Thankfully, skilled scientists and researchers labored diligently to develop and distribute treatments as well as vaccines to fight the coronavirus. However, there is no medication, treatment, or operation that can as easily "fix" the spiritual woes and maladies we face as a global society.

There is, however, a remedy for many of these ills—one that may seem surprising, because it flies in the face of our natural inclinations and intuitions. Nevertheless, its effects have been validated by scientists and men and women of faith alike.

I am referring to the healing power of gratitude.

Gratitude Is Key to Happiness

Writing for *Psychology Today*, Dr. Lisa Firestone proclaimed that "gratitude is perhaps the most important key to finding success and happiness in the modern day. Knowing what we appreciate in life means knowing who we are, what matters to us and what makes each day worthwhile."[1]

Dr. Robin Stern, cofounder and associate director for the Yale Center for Emotional Intelligence, concurs: "Sometimes it's hard in the midst of tremendous uncertainty and grief, anxiety and anger about what's happening, to feel grateful. But gratitude can be healing."[2]

New York Times columnist David Brooks has called gratitude "a sort of laughter of the heart."[3]

Ancient wisdom concurred with modern thought. The Roman

statesman and philosopher Cicero wrote that gratitude is "not only the greatest, but is also the parent of all the other virtues."

The book of Psalms is filled with admonitions to express gratitude. Here are just four of them:

"It is a good thing to give thanks unto the Lord."[4]

"O give thanks unto the Lord; for he is good."[5]

"Come before his presence with thanksgiving."[6]

"O give thanks unto the God of gods: for his mercy endureth for ever."[7]

Jesus Christ frequently expressed gratitude. Before raising Lazarus from the dead, before miraculously multiplying loaves and fishes, and before passing the cup to His disciples at the Last Supper, the Savior prayed and gave thanks to God, His Heavenly Father. No wonder the Apostle Paul later declared, "In every thing give thanks."[8]

When the prophet Nephi was tied to the mast of a ship and suffered there so long that his ankles and wrists were "swollen exceedingly," and though a violent storm threatened to plunge their ship into the depths of the sea, Nephi wrote, "I did look unto my God, and I did praise him all the day long; and I did not murmur against the Lord because of mine afflictions."[9]

While confronted with the hideous conditions in the Liberty Jail, the Prophet Joseph Smith described their state in a letter to Emma: "I believe it is now about five months and six days since I have been under the grimace of a guard, night and day, and within the walls, grates, and screeching iron doors of a lonesome, dark, dirty prison. . . . Let what will become of us, we cannot get into a worse hole than this is."[10]

And yet, in the midst of these subhuman conditions, Joseph also recorded these inspired words: "Dearly beloved brethren, let us *cheerfully* do all things that lie in our power; and then may we stand still, with the utmost assurance, to see the salvation of God, and for his arm to be revealed."[11]

Scripture and history are replete with examples of men and women who have risen above difficult circumstances and still praised the Lord.

During my ten decades of living, I have concluded that *counting* our blessings is far better than *recounting* our problems. Rather than just enumerating our trials, we can pray to understand them. We can pray to see them as opportunities for growth, even for our transformation. Therefore, no matter our situation, showing gratitude for our privileges and blessings, as well as for our afflictions and trials, is a fast-acting, long-lasting emotional and spiritual prescription.

Harvard professor and *New York Times* columnist Arthur Brooks wrote that gratitude is "common sense: Choosing to focus on good things makes you feel better than focusing on bad things. As my teenage kids would say, 'Thank you, Captain Obvious.' In the slightly more elegant language of the Stoic philosopher Epictetus, 'He is a man of sense who does not grieve for what he has not, but rejoices in what he has.'"[12]

Gratitude may not come easily. We may be operating under the notion that unless everything is going well in our lives, we have nothing for which to be grateful. But the opposite is actually true. Challenges and even hardships are not only part of life; they are part of a *good* life! One of our quests here in mortality is to learn how to solve problems and deal with setbacks.

If we would take a few minutes each day to do what many do on Thanksgiving Day—when we gather with loved ones and friends and each takes a turn to express gratitude for various blessings—I am certain that our feelings about life as well as our relationships with others would improve exponentially.

Gratitude helps us focus on the positive elements in our lives rather than obsess about our challenges—which we all have. Even in times of disappointment, there is always something for which we can be grateful.

Perhaps this is why, in 1789, U.S. President George Washington first declared "a day of public thanksgiving and prayer to be observed by acknowledging with grateful hearts the many signal favors of Almighty God especially by affording them an opportunity peaceably to establish a form of government for their safety and happiness."[13]

Gratitude Restores Perspective

Does gratitude spare us from sorrow, sadness, grief, and pain? No, but it does soothe our feelings and provide us with a greater perspective on the purpose and joys of life.

Despite the disappointments and personal losses I have experienced in my life, I am eternally grateful for so many things. During each time of loss and deep sadness, the Lord has blessed me with His support and that of family members and friends to buoy me up.

I, of course, am not alone in finding solace after experiencing loss. Horatio G. Spafford was a successful attorney and real estate investor who lost his fortune in the great Chicago fire of 1871. Around the same time, scarlet fever took the life of his four-year-old son.

He and his family were devastated. Believing that a vacation would give them time to mourn, he sent his wife and four daughters on a ship to England, planning to join them after he finished some business at home. While crossing the Atlantic, however, the ship carrying his family members sunk. His wife survived, but his four daughters drowned. Upon arriving in England, she sent a telegram to her husband that read: "Saved alone. What shall I do?" I can only try to imagine the grief Horatio must have felt.

Horatio immediately set sail for England. The captain of his ship was aware of the tragedy in Horatio's family. When they passed over the place where his family's ship had sunk, the captain made him aware of the location. As Horatio tried to grapple with his grief, words of comfort filled his heart and mind. Those words have since become the text for a beloved hymn, one verse of which reads:

When peace like a river, attendeth my way,
When sorrows like sea-billows roll;
Whatever my lot, Thou hast taught me to say
It is well, it is well, with my soul.

In his own way, Horatio Spafford's words express a remarkable kind of deep gratitude, even amidst great trial.

Gratitude Heals

Wednesday, November 7, 2018, was a normal fall day in Paradise, California. But early the following morning, tragedy struck early and quickly. A faulty electric transmission line sparked a fire along Camp Creek Road in northern California's Butte County, and a strong east wind drove the fire downhill through several towns. A literal firestorm formed in the foothill town of Paradise, and what was known as the Camp Fire quickly became the deadliest wildfire to hit California to that point in time.

The Camp Fire burned more than 150,000 acres and drove 52,000 people from their homes. Most heartbreaking of all, more than eighty people lost their lives. The sadness was inexpressible.

A few weeks later, in January 2019, Wendy and I visited Paradise, California, to comfort those affected by this tragedy. When we scheduled our visit, we did not know that just forty hours prior to leaving for California, we would lose a daughter to cancer. We flew to California with heavy hearts but looking forward to focusing on something other than our own sadness.

In Paradise, we witnessed utter devastation. The foundations of home after home were littered with piles of ash and the scarred remains of random items that had somehow escaped the inferno. It was a scene from a horror movie. Families were homeless, businesses were gone, and children were haunted by the day they fled for their lives.

But in Paradise we also saw something else. The Camp Fire revealed the best of humanity—first responders racing to help others as their own homes burned, families helping older neighbors out of harm's way, friends putting their own lives in danger to make sure that others were safe, and residents of neighboring cities working tirelessly to help those who were suddenly homeless. The expressions of gratitude for those who came to the rescue were endless.

We experienced that same compassion ourselves. As we tried to comfort those still reeling from the upheaval in their lives, they seemed more concerned about how *we* were doing in *our* time of loss. We flew home filled with the healing balm of gratitude for the goodness of so many.

There Is So Much for Which to Be Grateful

Regardless of the circumstances in our lives, we can find heavenly gifts and blessings for which we can be grateful.

We can give thanks for the beauties of the earth and the majesty of the heavens that give us an inkling of the vastness of eternity.

We can give thanks for the gift of life, for our amazing bodies and minds that allow us to grow and learn and enjoy life.

We can give thanks for art, literature, and music that nurture our souls, bring depth and richness to life, and invite the Spirit to be with us.

We can give thanks for our families, friends, and loved ones who fill our lives with a richness we could not experience any other way.

We can give thanks for the chance to help, cherish, and serve one another, which makes life so much more meaningful.

We can give thanks for the Restoration of the gospel of Jesus Christ with all of the knowledge, privileges, Godly power, and gifts it contains.

We can even give thanks for our trials, from which we learn and develop strengths we would not acquire otherwise.

Most of all, we can give thanks to God, the Father of our spirits. This truth reminds us that we are all brothers and sisters—one great global family.

And always we can give thanks for our Savior, Jesus Christ, whose infinite Atonement makes it possible for us to have access to His healing, strengthening power. When we bind ourselves to God and to Jesus Christ by making covenants with Them, we need never feel alone.

Three Invitations to Express Gratitude

As a doctor, I know the value of good therapy. So, may I prescribe three activities to help you *experience* the healing power of gratitude.

First, I invite you to turn social media into your own personal *gratitude journal*. Rather than complaining about things you don't like and criticizing the people with whom you disagree, begin posting about *what* you are grateful for, *who* you are grateful for, and *why* you are grateful. Try it and see if you don't feel happier. See if your perspective of life and of your relationships doesn't broaden and brighten.

Imagine the impact we would have if we transformed social media into a vehicle for expressing gratitude and looking for the good in others. Perhaps this could help fulfill, at least in part, the promise God gave to Father Abraham, that through his descendants, "all families of the earth [shall] be blessed."[14]

Second, look for opportunities to thank those closest to you for the difference they make in your life. This could start with family members and dear friends. But imagine how surprised a teacher, coach, or flight attendant might be to receive a simple expression of your gratitude. You may be surprised at how easy it is to light up someone's day.

Third, every day thank God, your Heavenly Father, in the name of Jesus Christ, for your many blessings—including the blessing of your trials and His help to you through those trials. Jesus Christ taught His disciples to pray by first expressing gratitude to God and then petitioning Him for the things we need. Prayers of gratitude bring forth miracles.

Prayer is your sacred, private time to talk with your Heavenly Father. Notice what happens when you thank Him for His Son, the priesthood, the gift of the Holy Ghost, the ministering of angels, the Book of Mormon, temples, fasting, repentance, forgiveness, and for prophets to lead and guide you. You might express thanks for any and every opportunity to learn and grow, to educate your mind and heart, and for those who teach and mentor you. Let God know how truly grateful you are for life itself.

As you make gratitude part of every day, and as you become more intentional in expressing gratitude to God and to others, you will be amazed at how optimistic you feel about your life and your future.

Gratitude Is a Demonstration of Faith

When we express gratitude in *all* circumstances, we are following the example of our Savior, Jesus Christ. In the Garden of Gethsemane, He pledged, "Father, if thou be willing, remove this cup from me: nevertheless not my will, but thine, be done."[15]

True gratitude is an expression of faith, hope, *and* charity. It shows faith in the Father's great plan of salvation, confidence in His omnipotence, and assurance that He will overrule for our good.

The Prophet Joseph Smith wrote a spirited epistle to the Church during a period of time that was otherwise filled with personal challenges. Yet his exuberance exemplifies how we might look to the future: "Shall we not go on in so great a cause?" he wrote. "Go forward and not backward. Courage, . . . and on, on to the victory! Let your hearts rejoice, and be exceedingly glad."[16]

An attitude of gratitude, to Heavenly Father and to those around us, will almost certainly allow your spirit to rejoice.

Alma's instruction to his son Helaman guides us today: "Counsel with the Lord in all thy doings, and he will direct thee for good; yea, when thou liest down at night lie down unto the Lord, that he may watch over you in your sleep; and when thou risest in the morning let thy heart be full of thanks unto God; and if ye do these things, ye shall be lifted up at the last day."[17]

Gratitude is medicine for the soul. Gratitude heals.

CHAPTER 10

KNOW THAT WITH GOD YOU CAN ACCOMPLISH THE IMPOSSIBLE

God uses the unlikely to accomplish the impossible.

How often have you been inspired by someone who accomplished something that seemed utterly impossible? Perhaps it was someone who overcame incredible odds or one who persisted to make an important discovery after previous failures. Perhaps it was someone who felt totally unprepared to accomplish an ominous task, and yet did it.

I have witnessed this phenomenon again and again and have even experienced it repeatedly myself—so much so that *I can say without reservation that the Lord uses the unlikely to accomplish the impossible.*

Some years ago, I found myself teaching a woman from Great Britain about the Restoration. She liked much of what she heard, but she had a difficult time accepting the idea that God the Father and His Son Jesus Christ would have appeared to a fourteen-year-old boy and subsequently restored His Church. She told me that it would certainly be easier for her to believe and accept the Restoration if God and His Son had appeared to the Archbishop of Canterbury!

The fact that the Father and the Son appeared to an untitled youth is one of many remarkable aspects of the Restoration. By worldly standards, and the best thinking of theologians, the young Joseph Smith was an unlikely candidate to be chosen as the Lord's prophet. He had not graduated from a prominent divinity school, nor did he have much formal schooling of any kind. But none of that mattered, because God chose the young Joseph to be the instrument through whom He restored the gospel of Jesus Christ.

This pattern of using the unlikely to accomplish the impossible is one that God has used repeatedly throughout history. Who would have believed David could slay Goliath with a stone and sling?[1] Or that with the crudest of tools, the young Nephi could build a ship "not after the manner of men"[2] that, despite his brothers' constant heckling, proved seaworthy enough to carry Lehi's family across the ocean to the promised land?[3] Truly, God chooses the weak things of the world to do His mighty work,[4] and "by small and simple things are great things brought to pass; and small means in many instances doth confound the wise."[5]

God has always asked His covenant children to do difficult things. Abrahamic tests did not stop with Abraham.

As the Lord explained to Joseph Smith: "[You] must needs be chastened and tried, even as Abraham, who was commanded to offer up his only son. For all those who will not endure chastening . . . cannot be sanctified."[6]

The seemingly impossible tasks we each face are literally stepping stones to sanctification.

The Lord Uses the Weak to Work Miracles

I know how unnerving it is to be asked to do something that seems far beyond your native capacity. I had been a member of the Quorum of the Twelve Apostles just nineteen months when President Spencer W. Kimball passed away. In the first meeting of the First Presidency and Quorum of the Twelve following President Ezra Taft Benson's ordination as President of the Church, President Benson gave new assignments to the Twelve.

His assignment for me was startling: "You are to be responsible for all of the affairs of the Church in Europe and Africa, with a special assignment to open up the nations in Eastern Europe that are now under the yoke of Communism for the preaching of the gospel."

My immediate thought was, "Are you sure Dallin shouldn't have this assignment? He is an attorney. I am a heart surgeon. I know how to open hearts, but what do I know about opening countries?" Thankfully, I did not express these thoughts. But at that moment, climbing Mt. Everest looked to be about as realistic.

Europe has always been important to the Church. The steady stream of early converts from the British Isles and Scandinavia infused irreplaceable strength into the Church during its formative years. However, in 1985, more of Europe lay behind the Iron Curtain than not: Poland, Hungary, Czechoslovakia, Romania, Bulgaria, Albania, Macedonia, Yugoslavia, Estonia, Lithuania, Latvia, the German Democratic Republic, and all of the USSR were under the yoke of Communism.

That unforgettable day when President Benson issued this new assignment came roughly nineteen months *before* U.S. President Ronald Reagan would declare, on June 12, 1987, "Mr. Gorbachev, tear down this wall," and four years *before* the Berlin Wall would fall on November 9, 1989.

There were far more countries in Europe that had *not* recognized the Church than had. I scarcely knew where to begin. Words from the Apostle Paul rushed to mind: "God hath chosen the foolish things of the world to confound the wise; and God hath chosen the weak things of the world to confound the things which are mighty."[7] I felt like a living object lesson of that truth.

During the next several years, I worked hard and tried my best. I made dozens of trips to Eastern Europe and to the former Soviet Union, as well as countless visits to Washington, D.C., to meet with ambassadors and other dignitaries who could help open doors for me throughout Europe.

In nations that were largely atheistic, I was never wanted and rarely welcome. Many governmental leaders, at least initially, wouldn't even give an appointment to a religious man who professed faith in God. In fact, at the time, believers were being imprisoned and even executed in some countries.

Little by little, however, we made a little progress here and there. Gratefully, as it turned out, many Eastern European countries kept meticulous records about visits from foreigners. In some countries, I was on record as an American heart surgeon who, as a volunteer, had lectured and taught there.

Paired with Elder Hans B. Ringger of the Seventy, a Swiss engineer and architect, our partnership disarmed some leaders. We were a much different team than were leaders from other faith groups. And our requests were different. Many other religions were asking for money. We were asking for permission to strengthen their citizens through the truths and blessings of the restored gospel of Jesus Christ. In country after country, one appointment at a time, we labored diligently to introduce the Church to dignitaries in charge. We did this in Russia, Ukraine, Romania, Bulgaria, Belarus, Czechoslovakia, Hungary, Yugoslavia, Estonia, Poland, Armenia, and the German Democratic Republic.

Each country presented different challenges. We worked and prayed as diligently as we knew how. When all was said and done, we turned to the Lord to make up the difference. Again and again, He did.

Of the dozens of experiences that I could mention, I will cite examples from just two countries—Hungary and Romania.

First, Hungary. On April 19, 1987—Easter Sunday—I dedicated Hungary for the preaching of the gospel. Two days later, Elder Ringger and I met with Dr. Imre Miklos, chairman of the Council of Religious Affairs. Our appointment did not begin well. Dr. Miklos asked if I knew David M. Kennedy. I responded that I did and that he was a good friend. "Well, I hate him!" Miklos blustered. I thought to myself, "No one who knows David Kennedy hates him, but strike one!"

Unfortunately, our conversation deteriorated from there. Though I tried to explain that we had come to his country to begin a friendship, the tension was almost suffocating. Our translators were in a battle. Ours said that the translator for Dr. Miklos was not translating correctly.

In the midst of that contention, it occurred to me that I should tell him about praying for his country. I told him that on the Sunday just past, I had gone to Mount Gellert and offered an apostolic prayer that the Lord's Spirit would be poured out upon his beautiful land and its people, and that the country would prosper.

The room suddenly grew quiet. I could feel the presence of the Spirit of the Lord and witnessed the Spirit working on that man. A meeting planned for thirty minutes ended up lasting an hour and a half. At one point, I mentioned that I understood Hungary had one of the highest death rates in Europe from alcohol and explained that the Church had resources that might help him. Dr. Miklos was skeptical, but I invited him to call the minister of religious affairs in the German Democratic Republic. "You don't have to take my word for it," I told him. "The minister in the DDR has been dealing with members of our Church for decades. Talk to him."

Miklos made the call. Things did not change immediately, but over time Miklos became an ally. In fact, he turned to me when his wife became ill, and I facilitated the care needed for her heart condition. On June 14, 1988, Elder Ringger and I returned to Budapest for formal ceremonies that officially recognized the Church in Hungary.

Romania posed different challenges. Elder Ringger and I arrived in Bucharest with a scheduled appointment with the chief of protocol of the State Office of Religious Affairs. At his office, however, we were told that our meeting had been postponed for two days. Two days later we were supposed to be in Turkey, but we juggled our schedules and walked the streets of Bucharest during the interim.

Before long, we realized we were being followed. Repeatedly we were propositioned—by individuals attempting to exchange money on the black market, by lewd women, and by a host of other bad actors. We refused each offer and went to the circus instead.

When we reported back to the Office of Religious Affairs, we were asked why we hadn't gone to the U.S. Embassy. I told them that we also did not go to the Swiss Embassy because we had no business with either embassy. I stated that we were in Bucharest solely to meet with the Office of Religious Affairs. Throughout Eastern Europe, I often had to convince officials that I was not in their country as an American but rather as a representative of a worldwide church.

We did not make much progress on that first visit. It took a subsequent political coup to open the doors for another meeting in Romania, this time with the new head of religious affairs for the new government. This man happened to be a pediatrician, and when we arrived at his office, the waiting room was filled with crying babies and their mothers.

When we were ushered into this man's office, our conversation lasted just a few moments before he said, with some impatience, "If you really want to help me, you will leave my office immediately and get out of here." I told him that I understood, that I was a doctor also. I asked if he could tell me in one word how our Church could help him.

"Orphans," he said.

I promised that we could help. It took just one visit to a Romanian orphanage for me to understand just how urgent the situation was. Once back in Salt Lake City, I called upon experts from Church Social Services and BYU to provide resources and volunteers to address this issue.

My colleagues and I addressed other needs in Romania. We helped stock their depleted libraries, which made both teachers and students shout for joy. And when we learned that the new Romanian government needed help drafting a constitution, we found an expert to assist them.

Recognition for the Church in Romania, as well as every country in Eastern Europe, at first seemed impossible. Only rarely did scheduled meetings lead to positive results. However, we continued to travel to Europe, meeting with dignitaries and seeking the Lord's guidance to know what steps to take next. Each of us who were involved at various stages of these efforts were the most unlikely of servants to accomplish this work. It seemed impossible.

At the end of 1990, my assignments in the Quorum of the Twelve were changed, and I was relieved of the responsibility for

Europe. That assignment was transferred to then-Elder Dallin H. Oaks. On December 14, 1990, Elder Oaks and I reported to President Benson that the Church was now established in every country in Eastern Europe.

In only five years, the Lord had opened one door after another for us. We were the most unlikely of servants. He assisted us to accomplish what seemed impossible.

The Lord Loves Effort

Throughout this intense period of labor in Eastern Europe, I was reminded of several things. One of my learnings was that the Lord loves effort. *And He honors effort.* When we serve Him diligently, and give our best effort, the Lord steps in and makes up the difference between our effort and what is required.

Our Heavenly Father sent us here, in the latter part of these latter days, to be successful. He wants us to realize that "with God *nothing shall be impossible*."[8] Those who make covenants with Him and keep them are entitled, through their worthiness, to receive revelation, strength, and access to godly power to assist with righteous endeavors.

Our Faith Can Move Mountains

How can we do the impossible? How can we move the mountains in our lives?

Doing the impossible begins with faith. Every potential blessing of eternal significance, every miracle, and every triumph over something that seems impossible begins with faith. Allowing God to prevail in our lives begins with faith that He is willing to guide us. True repentance begins with faith that Jesus Christ has the power to cleanse, heal, and strengthen us.[9]

"Deny not the power of God," the prophet Moroni declared, "for he worketh by power, according to the faith of the children of men."[10] Truly, it is our faith that unlocks the power of God in our lives.

However, sometimes exercising faith can seem impossible. We may wonder if we can possibly muster enough faith to receive the blessings that we so desperately need. Alma taught us that the first step to break through our fear is simply to *experiment* upon the word and "exercise a *particle* of faith, yea, even if [we] can no more than desire to believe."[11] The phrase "particle of faith" reminds me of the Lord's biblical promise that if we "have faith as a *grain of mustard seed*," we shall be able to "say unto this mountain, Remove hence to yonder place; and it shall remove; and nothing shall be *impossible* unto [us]."[12]

The Lord understands our mortal weakness. We all falter at times. But He also knows of our great potential. The mustard seed starts small but grows into a tree large enough for birds to nest in its branches. The mustard seed represents a small but *growing* faith.[13]

The Lord does not require perfect faith for us to have access to His perfect power. But He does ask us to believe, to keep drawing closer to Him, and to act in faith.

Start Today to Increase Your Faith

Our challenge is to *start today* to increase our faith. Through faith, Jesus Christ will increase our ability to move the mountains in our lives. Our opportunity is to exercise the kind of faith that will help us accomplish the impossible, whatever that may entail.

Our mountains may be loneliness, doubt, illness, weakness with a particular temptation, or other personal challenges. Our mountains will vary, and yet the answer to each challenge is to increase our faith. This of course takes work. Remember, the Lord loves effort. Lazy learners and lax disciples will always struggle to muster even a particle of faith.

Faith takes work. Receiving revelation takes work. But "every one that asketh receiveth; and he that seeketh findeth; and to him that knocketh it shall be opened."[14] So ask, and then ask again.

God knows what will help our faith grow. Ask Him, and then ask again.

A nonbeliever might say that faith is for the weak. But this assertion overlooks the *power* of faith. Would the Savior's Apostles have continued to teach His doctrine after His death, at the peril of their lives, if they had doubted Him? Without faith, would Abinadi have suffered death by fire for refusing to deny what he knew to be true?[15] Without faith, would Ether have hidden in the cavity of a rock and Moroni endured years of loneliness when their lives could have been far more comfortable if they had only denounced what they believed?[16] Would Joseph and Hyrum Smith have suffered martyrs' deaths defending the Restoration of the Lord's Church unless they had a sure witness that it was true? Would tens of thousands of Saints have ventured out to cross a forbidding prairie had they not had faith that the gospel of Jesus Christ had been restored and that they were helping to build Zion?[17]

Faith is the power that enables us, who feel so unlikely, to accomplish the impossible. Faith is the power that helps each of us conquer our individual challenges and do the work the Lord requires us to do.

Miracles Come in All Forms

In 2019, Wendy and I had the privilege of traveling with Elder Gerrit W. Gong and his wife Sister Susan Gong on visits to Australia, New Zealand, Samoa, Tonga, Fiji, and Tahiti. Our trip was deeply rewarding as we traveled throughout the South Pacific. In Samoa, Tonga, Fiji, and Tahiti, those island nations had experienced heavy rains for days, so members in each location fasted and prayed that their outdoor meetings would be protected from the rain.

In Samoa, Fiji, and Tahiti, the rain stopped just as the meetings began. That was a miracle! However, in Tonga, the rain did *not* stop. Their miracle came in a different form: 13,000 faithful Saints came hours early to get a seat, waited patiently through a steady drizzle, and then sat through a very wet two-hour meeting.

Where was the greater faith? Where the rain stopped, or where it did not? In reality, we saw vibrant faith at work among *each* of those congregations of islanders—faith sufficient to stop the rain in some locations and faith requisite to persevere when the rain did not stop in another.

The mountains in our lives do not always move how or when we would like. But our faith will always propel us forward. Faith always increases our access to godly power.

Please know this: If everything and everyone else in the world whom you trust were to fail, Jesus Christ and His Church will never fail you. The Lord never slumbers, nor does He sleep.[18] He "is the same yesterday, today, and [tomorrow]."[19] He works miracles today, and He will work miracles tomorrow.[20]

He will work many of those miracles through our growing faith. For the Lord uses the unlikely to accomplish the impossible!

CHAPTER 11

HONOR YOUR BODY

The body is a sacred gift and should be treated like one.

My home state of Utah has some of the finest snow on earth. My first attempt at skiing as a boy involved long, wooden, single-groove skis and toe straps over my galoshes. The skier had no ability to turn. It was straight downhill, and because there were no ski lifts, every foot downhill meant climbing back up to ski down again. I was not very enamored with the sport.

Many years later, a neurosurgeon colleague offered to teach me how to really ski. At that point, skiing was an established sport. With ski lifts and more modern equipment, I advanced from trying to survive getting down the mountain to wanting to teach my children. My joy came from seeing their joy—first as they skied braced between my knees, and then as they quickly launched themselves into soloing. I skied for years with family and friends, and I grew to love the sport.

I skied until the day I became President of the Church, at age ninety-three, when my security officers insisted that I stop. They said they were no longer willing to risk having an erratic snowboarder crash into me, but I secretly believe they were tired of trying to keep up with me on those Black Diamond runs.

I have been blessed with good health, and I have been conscientious about taking care of my body. I have weighed myself every day for decades, and if I put on a pound or two, I cut back on my intake for a few days. Years of treating patients with heart maladies convinced me that the most important number to watch is one's weight.

As an aside, I am *not* advocating being model thin, going on extreme diets, or spending excessive amounts of time working out. A person's worth is not measured by their appearance. "For the Lord seeth not as man seeth; for man looketh on the outward appearance, but the Lord looketh on the heart."[1] I simply suggest that keeping your weight within a healthy range for your body type is important for long-term health.

The Wonder of the Human Body

It was the study of medicine that convinced me that God was real. The more I learned about the human body, the more I realized that only a Divine Being could have created something so magnificent.

As scientists, we do not know how two cells unite to form an embryo or how primitive cells differentiate to become a beating heart or a thinking brain. We just know that they do so according to a pattern established by our Heavenly Father.

I fear that the marvel and miracle of our physical bodies is too often underappreciated today. Probably most of us have wished at times that we were taller or thinner, had higher cheekbones or curlier hair. And yet, ponder the magnificence of what you see when you look in the mirror. Ignore the blemishes and see the miracle that is you! Each organ of your body is a wondrous gift from God.

For example, consider the jewel that is the human heart—a pump so remarkable that its power and durability is almost beyond comprehension. This tremendous organ pumps enough fluid every day to fill the equivalent of a 2,000-gallon railroad tank-car. Your heart has four tiny valves that open and close 100,000 times a day, over 36 million times a year, without any effort on your part.

These valves are as soft and billowy as a parachute, yet as tough as sinew. Unless altered by disease, heart valves are so rugged that they can stand this wear and tear for decades. No man-made material developed thus far can be flexed so frequently and for so long without breaking or wearing out.

One of the biggest problems researchers working to develop the first artificial hearts encountered was to find a material that could be folded and unfolded many times a day, day after day, without ultimate fatigue and fracture. The heart does enough mechanical work to lift a 150-pound person from the street up to the top of the Empire State Building every day. Yet in so doing, it consumes minute amounts of energy.

At the crest of the heart is an electrical transmitting center that sends signals down special circuits that cause all of the muscle fibers to contract together with a synchronized response that would be the envy of any conductor of a symphony orchestra.

The first artificial heart-lung machine we made occupied many square feet of space. The pump that our Creator made occupies a space about the size of your fist and does not need to be plugged into an electrical outlet. The power to your heart is provided, not by battery or cord, not by compressed air or by nuclear energy, but by a process known only to God.

Consider other properties of the body. The human brain with its countless combinations of recording, memory, storage, and retrieval systems serves as the headquarters for one's personality, character, and knowledge. The brain's capacity appears to be unlimited. The more it is stimulated and challenged, the more it seems able to do. The more we memorize music, equations, data, poetry, scriptures, and famous statements, the more our capacity for memorizing and retaining information increases.

What about our eyes? I remember the day I heard about a new camera that could autoregulate light and shutter speed settings. At the time, that advancement in technology seemed remarkable. Then I stood in front of a mirror, flashed a beam of light into my eye, and observed a brisk constriction of a perfectly round pupil. My eye responded instantly to regulate the intensity of light that could pass through a self-focusing lens to reach the sensitive retina in the back of the eye. We each own two "cameras," if you will, and when they function properly, they are finer than any camera money can buy.

Then consider the body's remarkable capacity to reproduce. Twenty-three chromosomes from both the father and the mother unite to make one new cell. These chromosomes contain thousands of genes. A marvelous process of genetic coding is established by which all the basic human characteristics of the unborn child are determined, and thus a new DNA complex is formed.

Approximately twenty-two days after those two germ cells unite, a little heart begins to beat. At twenty-six days, the circulation of blood begins. Cells multiply and divide, some being differentiated to become eyes that see or ears that hear, while still others are destined to become fingers, toes, and legs. The ability of the body to reproduce is magnificent and begins with conception.

The body also has the ability to protect itself from disease. I'll never forget watching some children drinking water that ran down the sidewalk in front of our home. The water carried mud from a neighbor's garden. I suppose the number of germs they ingested was incalculable, but not one child became ill. The defensive features of their bodies protected them.

I could go on and on. We could discuss the body's capacity to autoregulate on an almost infinite number of variables, beginning with temperature. We could explore the skin, which protects us against both extreme heat and cold, the ears, bones, adrenal glands, kidneys, lungs, and so on.

Perhaps most remarkably, the body has the power to heal. Broken bones heal. Wounds heal. Incisions and lacerations heal. A leak in the circulatory system will seal itself, whereas circulation systems outside the body do not have this power.

I gained appreciation for this miracle while working in the lab to create an artificial heart-lung machine. Whenever tubing in the machine would spring a leak, it meant long hours of cleaning up the lab. No artificial heart or heart-lung machine can repair itself. But the body can.

When I was a practicing physician, I felt that my ultimate responsibility was to determine if a patient's body had the ability to self-heal and get better over time, or if he or she needed to have medical help to initiate the healing process.

For example, a broken rib will get better over time. It will be painful for a while, but given time, the rib will heal with basically no help from a physician. A tumor on the rib, however, will not heal itself and will get worse without intervention.

Perhaps it is not a surprise that I, as a former physician, surgeon, and medical researcher, would go on and on about this remarkable gift we have each been given. But let me take my sense of awe about the body a step further, perhaps beyond what someone might learn through the practice of medicine.

The Body Is Actually a Temple

Jesus Christ Himself was the first to refer to His mortal body as a temple.[2] Later, the Apostle Paul asked the Corinthians, "Know ye not that ye are the temple of God, and that the Spirit of God dwelleth in you?" He then went on to declare that "if any man defile the temple of God, him shall God destroy; for the temple of God is holy, which temple ye are."[3]

I was a young surgical resident when these verses of scripture first caught my attention. Perhaps my intense study of the body made the Savior's and the Apostle Paul's words resonate with me in a special way. Over ensuing decades, this truth increased in meaning for me. In the eyes of our Heavenly Father and His Son Jesus Christ, our bodies are the equivalent of a temple. Therefore, it is our responsibility to treat our bodies with the care we give every house of the Lord. This is a lofty thought. Yet it is the truth—a truth that would help millions avoid self-inflicted health problems.

Our mortal bodies are literally gifts from God. Premortally, as spirit children of our Heavenly Father, we saw His body of flesh and bones and wanted to be like Him. His plan of salvation provided the way that we could receive a body and return to live with Him. The Proclamation on the Family puts the creation of the body in proper perspective: "Spirit sons and daughters knew and worshipped God as their Eternal Father and accepted His plan by which His children could obtain a physical body and gain earthly experience to progress toward perfection and ultimately realize their divine destiny as heirs of eternal life."[4] We in fact "shouted for joy"[5] at the prospects of the Father's plan.

The Prophet Joseph Smith put the importance of the body in perspective: "We came to this earth that we might have a body and present it pure before God in the celestial kingdom. The great principle of happiness consists in having a body. The devil has no body, and herein is his punishment. He is pleased when he can obtain the tabernacle of man."[6]

Consider the import of these truths articulated by Joseph Smith and their implications for how you treat your body. He taught that, first, we came here to obtain a body. Second, happiness is connected to having a body. Third, the adversary and those who followed him lost the right to have a body when they rebelled against the Father and the Son; thus, Satan is determined to have us misuse our bodies. Fourth, and perhaps most importantly, because we have a body, we have power over the adversary. Our will—especially when fortified by the Spirit—is stronger than the devil's. The only power the adversary has is power we relinquish to him, which we do every time we abuse our body in any way.

With this understanding as our doctrinal foundation, should it be any surprise that the adversary works so hard to tempt us to abuse, deface, and misuse our bodies? *Most sins involve the body.* These include abuse, of others or ourselves; violations of the law of chastity, or the misuse of the sacred power of procreation; addiction, whether it be to alcohol, drugs, pornography, food, sex, tobacco, or any other substance or practice that violates divine law. Even the defacing of our bodies through tattooing is an affront to our Maker.

How Should We View Our Bodies?

Through the ages, some without doctrinal understanding have tried to explain our existence by pretentious words such as *ex nihilo* (out of nothing). Others have deduced that, because of certain similarities between different forms of life, there has been a natural selection of the species, or organized evolution from one form to another. Still others have concluded that man came to be as a consequence of a "big bang" that resulted in the creation of our planet and life upon it.

I do not find such theories helpful. Could an explosion in a printing shop produce a dictionary? Could a dictionary heal its own torn pages or renew its worn corners or reproduce its own subsequent editions?

The only explanation for the creation of something so magnificent as the human body is that it was created by God. The body is an unspeakable gift that allows us to work, play, love, travel, help others, and test our endurance. It allows us to learn, grow, develop talents, gain knowledge that we can retain, and communicate with each other. I agree with the Apostle Paul. Our bodies are the equivalent of a temple and should be revered.

Starting today, what would change in your life if you treated your body as one of God's greatest creations? Would that knowledge change how you care for your body? Would it affect the way you use it and adorn it? Would it influence how you regard the bodies of others?

If we treated our bodies as temples, surely there would be less immodesty, less immorality, less abuse, less viewing of pornography, less overeating, less physical indulgence of any kind.

On the other hand, if we treated our bodies as temples, there would be more modesty, more self-discipline, more adherence to the Word of Wisdom, and more gratitude for and obedience to the law of chastity. Consider this: As we treat our bodies as temples, our bodies will radiate the light and love of Jesus Christ and we will receive "his image in [our] countenances."[7]

Understanding how precious the body is in the eyes of God helps us understand why physical and sexual abuse of women, children—or for that matter, anyone—is an abomination to God. He grieves whenever anyone is harmed. He mourns, as we all mourn, for any person who falls victim to the disgusting evil of abuse. Those who perpetrate these hideous acts, and defile or torment another's body, are not only accountable to the laws of man but will also face the wrath of Almighty God. Of that I am certain.

Now, an important note: No one has a perfect body, and the relentless pursuit of a perfect body will prove superficial at best and can actually lead to illness and even death, as in the case of anorexia and bulimia. A perfect body is not required to be happy or to enjoy the richness life has to offer. Caring for our bodies, on the other hand, will pay unending dividends.

Your body is a gift from God that makes it possible for you to complete your mortal probation and do all that your Heavenly Father needs you to do here on earth.

CHAPTER 12

LISTEN TO LATTER-DAY PROPHETS

The Lord speaks to us through His prophets.

One of the things I have learned in my life is that some of the greatest sources of security, and some of the most reliable sources of unassailable truth, are prophets of God. Considering the fact that I have served as a member of the Quorum of the Twelve Apostles since 1984, I am sure this statement does not come as a surprise. But I learned this truth long before my call to the Twelve.

During my life, I have learned that prophets see ahead. They see the harrowing dangers the adversary has placed, or will yet place, in our path. Prophets also foresee the grand possibilities awaiting those who listen to prophetic counsel with the intent to obey. Perhaps two experiences will illustrate my point of view.

In late 1965, I received an unexpected but intriguing invitation. The University of Chicago medical school made me a too-good-to-be-true offer to join their acclaimed university as professor of surgery and chairman of the Division of Cardiovascular and Thoracic

Surgery. Dantzel and I traveled to Chicago to assess the opportunity, and the school rolled out the red carpet. The opportunity seemed like a dream come true.

A young, highly respected law professor at the university by the name of Dallin H. Oaks, with his wife June, hosted us during our stay. We loved every moment with them and were overwhelmed by the university's generous offer.

Dantzel and I decided to accept the offer. Because I was serving as president of the Bonneville Stake in Salt Lake City, I told my high council that I would be moving. Brother Joseph Anderson—a member of our high council who was then serving as secretary to the First Presidency—pulled me aside after the meeting and suggested that I talk about this move with President David O. McKay. I couldn't imagine that the President of the Church would concern himself with the occupational move of a stake president, but Brother Anderson insisted that I talk with the prophet.

So, on December 14, 1965, I met with President McKay and told him about the Chicago offer. President McKay listened intently and asked many questions: Why were we considering the move? How many children did we have? What would this mean for them? Was this about fame or money? What impact would it have on my career? The prophet left no stone unturned.

I will never forget what happened next. President McKay leaned his head back on his chair and closed his eyes for a prolonged period of time. Finally, he opened his eyes and said, "Brother Nelson, it doesn't feel good to me. Your place is here in Salt Lake City. People will come from all over the world to you here. I don't think you should go to Chicago."

Though surprised by his counsel, we turned down the offer. Over the following years, everything President McKay said would happen did in fact occur. Our children prospered in Salt Lake City, and I did in fact have opportunities to influence the global cardiovascular surgical community.

Another interaction with a prophet of God helped spur my professional career further. In 1979, while serving as Sunday School General President, I was invited to attend a Regional Representatives' seminar during which President Spencer W. Kimball delivered a landmark address about opening the doors of nations that were then closed to the Church, including China. He challenged everyone present to study the Mandarin language so that we could communicate with the Chinese people.

That evening I asked Dantzel if she would be willing to study Mandarin with me. She immediately agreed, and we found a tutor to help us. Of course, we didn't learn to speak Mandarin very well, but we learned enough that, when I was invited the next year—through a series of highly unexpected events—to go to China as a visiting professor to teach open-heart surgery, I was in a position to accept the invitation.

I subsequently made many professional trips to China and made friends with many colleagues there. In fact, the year after I was called to the Quorum of the Twelve, I received an urgent request to go to China to perform open-heart surgery on a famous opera star there—a man regarded throughout China as a national treasure. I explained that my full-time ecclesiastical responsibility prevented me from fulfilling their petition, but the doctors in China pleaded with me to reconsider.

After discussing this request with my quorum president and the First Presidency, they encouraged me to make the trip. Gratefully, the operation was a success! That operation in China proved to be the last open-heart procedure I ever performed. It was in Jinan, China, on March 4, 1985.

Fast-forward thirty years later, to October 2015. Wendy and

I were invited to return to the Shandong University School of Medicine in Jinan. There we were overwhelmed when I was warmly welcomed as "an old friend" of China and reunited with surgeons I had taught thirty-five years earlier, as well as *their* students. The highlight of that visit was meeting the son and grandson of the opera star on whom I had operated. These remarkable experiences—and many more—were possible for one reason: I had heeded the counsel of a prophet to study Mandarin.

Heeding the words of prophets is one of our greatest sources of security in today's complex world. You may not always understand the reason for every declaration of a living prophet. But when you know a prophet is a prophet, you can approach the Lord in humility and faith and ask for your own witness about whatever His prophet has proclaimed.

Prophets Are Extraordinary Role Models

While there is much to learn from the considerable leadership abilities of men and women such as Joan of Arc, George Washington, Abraham Lincoln, Winston Churchill, Mahatma Gandhi, Mother Teresa, and many others, I believe that the finest leaders to walk the earth are prophets of God.

I have been blessed to know personally ten of the sixteen men who preceded me as President of the Church. I suppose that says more about my age than anything else. Nonetheless, I have learned invaluable lessons from each of them. May I share a few leadership principles I have learned from four of these remarkable men?

Joseph Fielding Smith

President Joseph Fielding Smith, the tenth President of the Church, lived just a few houses away from my boyhood home. His two youngest sons were my friends. They often invited me into their home, and President Smith was always welcoming.

When I was called in 1971 to be the General President of the Sunday School, President Smith was President of the Church. Dantzel and I accompanied him later that year to the first area conference, held in Manchester, England. There I observed a powerful lesson in leadership as President Smith asked for reports from General Authorities who had gathered prior to the conference.

After each report, President Smith stood and expressed his love and desire to help. I was struck by the power of this leader as he expressed confidence in these General Authorities. After the area conference, when we complimented President Smith on his excellent message, he simply replied, "I did not come here to fail."[1]

That statement has lingered with me through the years. President Smith had faith that the Lord would guide those proceedings. Just as President Smith did not go to England to fail, so our Heavenly Father sent each of us here to earth in this final dispensation to succeed. President Smith taught me an important lesson about the power of leaders to encourage, strengthen, and instill confidence in those they serve.

Ezra Taft Benson

President Ezra Taft Benson had been a member of the Quorum of the Twelve for only two years when, in December 1945, in the aftermath of World War II, President George Albert Smith called him to preside over the European Mission. Conditions in Europe were severe. During a ten-month mission of love to members whose lives had been upended by war, Elder Benson traveled throughout war-torn Germany, Poland, Czechoslovakia, and Scandinavia to distribute food, clothing, and bedding to suffering Saints. He repeatedly faced what seemed to be insurmountable odds. Again and again, he demonstrated "undaunted faith in the power of the Lord to overcome obstacles."[2]

Forty years later, in November 1985, when President Benson assigned me as a junior member of the Twelve to open the doors of countries in Eastern Europe, I felt unprepared for the assignment. But how could I not do as he had done? His example propelled me to work as hard as I could and then wait for the Lord to extend His miraculous helping hand.

We can learn much from President Benson, who for eight years served concurrently as an Apostle and the secretary of agriculture in U.S. President Dwight D. Eisenhower's Cabinet. How did he manage such an impossible workload, with dual priorities that sometimes conflicted? These are his words: "I work as hard as I can and do everything within my power. And I try to keep the commandments. Then I let the Lord make up the difference."[3] Those are words to live by.

Gordon B. Hinckley

President Gordon B. Hinckley was a dynamic leader whose tutoring in Church governance was unique. Prior to serving as the fifteenth President of the Church, he had been a counselor to three previous Presidents. Upon returning from his mission as a young man to England, he worked for the Church in various capacities, always under the direction of the First Presidency and Quorum of the Twelve. Repeatedly he was asked to solve significant challenges. For example, President David O. McKay assigned Brother Hinckley to determine how to commit the endowment ordinance to film so that the endowment could be presented in multiple languages.

President Hinckley was a communicator *par excellence*. He spoke confidently about the gospel with everyone from seasoned journalists to world leaders. I witnessed him soften the heart of Mikhail

Gorbachev, former president of the Soviet Union, who initially resisted an invitation to meet with President Hinckley in *his* office at Church headquarters. (Gorbachev wanted President Hinckley to come to Gorbachev's hotel room.) However, when the two subsequently met at Church headquarters, President Hinckley pointed out the beautiful Circassian walnut paneling in the First Presidency council room. Mr. Gorbachev was captivated because that wood came from the region of his birthplace in Russia! His mood warmed immediately.

President Hinckley was unfailingly optimistic, an outgrowth of his faith in the Lord. During nearly thirteen years as President, he led the Church through a period of innovation, including the design of smaller temples, the building of the Conference Center, the announcement of 79 new temples, and the dedication or rededication of 95 of the 124 temples then in operation. President Hinckley's vision knew no bounds.

President Hinckley was fearless in proclaiming the future. Consider his prophetic words: "This cause [of Christ] will roll on in majesty and power to fill the earth. Doors now closed to the preaching of the gospel will be opened. The Almighty, if necessary, may have to shake the nations to humble them and cause them to listen to the servants of the living God. Whatever is needed will come to pass."[4] President Hinckley inspired us to "try a little harder to be a little better."[5]

Thomas S. Monson

President Thomas S. Monson was called to be a bishop at age twenty-two in a ward that included some eighty widows. He was then called to be an Apostle at the age of thirty-six. He lived his life according to the motto, which he repeated to me more than once:

"If the Lord needs something done, I want Him to know that He can count on Tom Monson to do it."

President Monson showed us how to reach out and rescue the one. He taught us by example that taking care of people is more important than meetings or schedules. Throughout his life, President Monson took random routes home at the end of a long day's work—sometimes stopping at a hospital to comfort someone in distress and other times feeling led to a specific home to visit. Often his unexpected knock on a door was met with a tearful person saying, "How did you know it was the anniversary of our daughter's death?" or "How did you know today was my birthday?"

President Monson's life consistently exemplified both the first and second great commandments—to love God with our whole souls and to love God's children as ourselves.

We can learn a lot from studying how prophets choose to live their lives.

Joseph Smith's Unparalleled Example

There is no latter-day prophet from whom we can learn more than the Prophet of this dispensation—the Prophet Joseph Smith. I marvel at all he accomplished in his relatively short life. His remarkable achievements were facilitated by the matchless power of Heavenly Father, the Lord Jesus Christ, and a host of heavenly beings.

In particular, Joseph Smith's experiences are evidence of the Lord's willingness to reveal Himself and His will to His prophets.

As we know, the Restoration began with the First Vision. In response to Joseph's prayer in 1820, Heavenly Father and His Son, Jesus Christ, appeared to the boy Joseph. They told him to join none of the current churches and "[promised] that the fulness of the gospel should at some future time be made known unto [him]."[6]

In addition to the First Vision, we know of at least *nine* other occasions when Joseph saw the Father *or* the Son. Four of these visions included both the Father *and* the Son, while the Savior appeared to the Prophet another five times by Himself.[7]

Two of these sublime manifestations of the Father and the Son are canonized in sections 76 and 137 of the Doctrine and Covenants.[8] Four years later in the nearly completed Kirtland Temple, Joseph "beheld the celestial kingdom of God" and the "blazing throne of God, whereon was seated the Father and the Son."[9] The other appearances of the Father and the Son occurred at a conference in Kirtland in 1831 and at the School of the Prophets.[10]

As stated earlier, Joseph Smith saw the Lord Jesus Christ on at least five additional occasions. One of those was in 1831 during a meeting at Isaac Morley's farm, and another in 1833, while Joseph was setting apart his father as Patriarch to the Church. The other three appearances occurred in the Kirtland Temple in the days surrounding its dedication, including the remarkable vision recorded in Doctrine and Covenants section 110.

On that occasion, Joseph Smith and Oliver Cowdery "saw the Lord standing upon the breastwork of the pulpit." They heard the Lord declare His personal identity, saying, "I am the first and the last; I am he who liveth, I am he who was slain; I am your advocate with the Father."[11]

In addition to these transcendent experiences with the Father and the Son, Joseph was visited by, or saw in vision, dozens of ancient prophets and angels.[12] Joseph personally interacted with "divers angels, from . . . Adam down to the present time, all declaring their dispensation, their rights, their keys, their honors, their majesty and glory, and the power of their priesthood."[13]

Through these remarkable experiences, the Prophet came to understand that heavenly knowledge transcends worldly knowledge. On one occasion, he declared, "Could you gaze into heaven five minutes, you would know more than you would by reading all that ever was written on the subject."[14]

President George Q. Cannon, a counselor to four Church Presidents,[15] said: "[Joseph] had vision after vision in order that his mind might be fully saturated with a knowledge of the things of God, and that he might comprehend the great and holy calling that God had bestowed upon him. In this respect he stands unique. There is no man in this dispensation [who] can occupy the station that he, Joseph did, God having reserved him and ordained him for that position, and bestowed upon him the necessary power."[16]

The Angel Moroni figured prominently in Joseph's early tutoring, making at least twenty visits to him in the 1820s.[17] At the time of Moroni's first visit, Joseph was only seventeen years old. In 1823, Moroni's first three visits occurred in rapid succession through the night in the upper story of the Smith's log home. "[Moroni] said there was a book deposited, written upon gold plates, giving an account of the former inhabitants of this continent, and . . . the fulness of the everlasting Gospel was contained in it,"[18] Joseph recorded.

Later, a vision was opened to Joseph's mind showing him "the place where the plates were deposited."[19] After going to the hill and uncovering the stone cavity, Joseph beheld the plates but was forbidden to remove them. He was instructed to meet Moroni at the hill one year to the date later.

Annual interviews took place atop the hill. These were sacred opportunities for Moroni to impart "instruction and intelligence" to Joseph regarding how the Lord's "kingdom was to be conducted in the last days."[20] During this time Joseph incrementally began to understand what Moroni meant when he told Joseph that "God had a work for [him] to do."[21]

Moroni remained in contact with Joseph throughout the duration of the translation of the Book of Mormon until he permanently reclaimed the plates. Moroni's visits prepared Joseph for future communications with heavenly beings.

Joseph Smith's Heavenly Tutoring

President John Taylor taught that Joseph Smith was acquainted with "such men . . . as Abraham, Isaac, Jacob, Noah, Adam, Seth, Enoch, and Jesus and the Father, and the apostles that lived on this continent as well as those who lived on the [Asian] continent."[22]

Other sources[23] confirm that Joseph was tutored by Old Testament prophets; all the New Testament Apostles, including Paul; and Book of Mormon prophets, including Nephi, Alma, Mormon, and the twelve Nephite disciples. Likewise, Joseph and others saw numerous unnamed angels during the Kirtland Temple dedication and in the following week, as part of the promised endowment "with power from on high."[24]

Many of these experiences are not captured in the scriptures, but various accounts[25] indicate that Joseph saw in vision or was visited by some sixty angels during his lifetime. John the Baptist and Peter, James, and John restored the keys of priesthood authority.[26] Others, such as Moses, Elias, and Elijah, also committed priesthood keys to Joseph.[27]

These divine interactions with angels were so frequent that President John Taylor observed that Joseph "seemed to be as familiar with these people as we are with one another." He believed that Joseph's familiarity with the ancients was necessary "because [Joseph] had to introduce . . . the dispensation of the fulness of times, . . .

—the dispensation in which all other dispensations are merged or concentrated."[28]

Joseph's unique calling required repeated tutoring so that he could establish the firm foundation of the Lord's Church that his successors would need so that they could accomplish the Lord's purposes in the future.

Joseph Smith and Latter-day Scripture

Now consider Joseph Smith's role as the revelator of latter-day scripture. Through the Prophet Joseph Smith we have received more pages of scripture than we have from any other prophet from the beginning of time!

He translated the Book of Mormon from an unknown language into the English language "by the gift and power of God,"[29] and he did this in one single draft without the advantage of modern technology!

I have examined surviving pages from the original manuscript, inscribed by the hand of Oliver Cowdery. The original manuscript is largely free from strikeouts and changes. This fact is stunning to me, especially when I consider the multiple iterations I generate for each message I give.

The Book of Mormon is tangible, irrefutable evidence of Joseph Smith's foreordained designation as the prophet of this dispensation.

Additionally, Joseph Smith received by revelation all but three of the 138 sections of the Doctrine and Covenants, often in the face of extreme adversity and persecution. These revelations were received in New York, Pennsylvania, Ohio, Missouri, Massachusetts, and Illinois. The Doctrine and Covenants proclaims the doctrine; establishes the administrative structure of the Church; and explains the keys, authority, and power of the priesthood in more detail than any other book of scripture.

Shortly after the Church was formally recognized, Joseph was directed to begin working on what we refer to as the Joseph Smith Translation of the Bible. He regarded this translation, this revelation, as part of his calling as prophet, seer, and revelator. This work was an important part of the Prophet's charge to restore the "many plain and precious things taken away from the [Bible]."[30]

The Pearl of Great Price includes the books of Moses and Abraham. These books also came by revelation. Think of the sacred truths taught in these books written by these two prophets, who were also heads of dispensations.

Through Joseph Smith, the Lord brought forth scriptures that He knew were necessary for His disciples to understand. These latter-day scriptures teach of God's eternal plan of happiness and of His covenant path to eternal glory.

The Significance of Latter-day Prophets

In considering what I have learned during a century of living about prophets, I have chosen to focus on the Prophet Joseph Smith and some of the Presidents of the Church whom I have known personally. I have done so for two reasons: first, to bear my witness that Joseph Smith is the prophet of this last dispensation. A testimony of the Prophet Joseph's pivotal role in the Restoration is a foundational pillar in anyone's testimony of the restored gospel of Jesus Christ.

Second, to testify that I have experienced for myself the privileges and blessings that come from heeding the words and counsel of latter-day prophets. Listening to prophets has literally changed the course of my life.

I have been blessed to serve in the Quorum of the Twelve under five Presidents of the Church. It has been my joy to watch each President seek, receive, and respond to direction from the Head of the Church, Jesus Christ.

Now, as I serve as President of the Church, I can speak from my own experience. I testify that our Savior always has instructed and inspired His prophets, and He always will. No one cares more about His Church than He does. Jesus Christ actively guides His prophets, seers, and revelators. Of this I bear personal witness.

PART 4

LAWS FOR WALKING THE COVENANT PATH

CHAPTER 13

IMMERSE YOURSELF IN THE WORD

The scriptures are a latter-day survival guide.

When Dantzel and I were married, no one would have called us scriptural experts. However, we loved the Lord and were obedient to His commandments. As a couple, we were drawn to Matthew 6:33 and adopted it as our guide: "Seek ye first the kingdom of God, and his righteousness; and all these things shall be added unto you." Thus, we commenced our marriage, not worrying about what we would buy or where we would live.

Years later, after we had finished my education and were in the midst of a busy surgical practice and raising a large family, I said to Dantzel one day, "I am not making any spiritual progress. Would it be okay with you if I got up an hour earlier each day to study the scriptures and to learn to play the organ?"

Thus began my morning routine of getting up at 4:30 a.m. to study and practice. I should note that I wore earphones connected to the organ so the family could sleep beyond 4:30 a.m. Little did I know that I would serve as organist for the weekly temple meetings of the First Presidency and Quorum of the Twelve for thirty years.

Those early morning hours of immersion in the scriptures were precious. Such regular study was spiritual food for me and proved to be the best way to prepare for my intense days in the operating room.

The Scriptures Point Us to Jesus Christ

I have already detailed how several verses in the Doctrine and Covenants propelled my research career. From that time on, I began to realize how relevant scriptures were to me personally.

First and foremost, the scriptures are relevant because they teach us about Jesus Christ, His mission and gospel, and His Atonement and Resurrection—which changed the course of history, fulfilled the plan of salvation, and made both salvation and exaltation a possibility for all. The scriptures lead us to "talk of Christ," "rejoice in Christ," and know where we may look for a remission of our sins.[1]

During a January 2017 worldwide devotional for young adults, I challenged those viewing the broadcast to increase their testimony of the Savior by doing four things: 1) study everything Jesus said and did as recorded in the Old Testament, for He is the Jehovah of the Old Testament; 2) study the Savior's laws as recorded in the New Testament, for He is its Christ; 3) study the Savior's doctrine as recorded in the Book of Mormon, for there is no book of scripture in which His mission and ministry are more clearly revealed; and 4) study His words as recorded in the Doctrine and Covenants, for He continues to teach His people in this dispensation.

I promised those listening that if they would learn all they could about Jesus Christ, their love for Him and for God's laws would grow beyond what they could currently imagine. I also promised them that their ability to turn away from sin would increase and they would be better able to walk away from the entertainment and entanglements of those who mock followers of Jesus Christ. What I did not mention to the young adults was that I was in the middle of completing these assignments myself.

On December 1, 2016, I had obtained a new set of scriptures and proceeded with the same assignments I would subsequently give to the young adults the following month, in January 2017. When I finished the assignment six weeks later, I had looked up and marked more than 2,200 citations from the Bible, the Book of Mormon, and the Doctrine and Covenants.

Accomplishing this assignment was thrilling! I told Wendy that I felt like a different man! I felt a renewed devotion to the Lord. I have devoted much of my one hundred years to learning about the Savior, but I cannot remember another time when I learned as much about Him as I did during that unique six-week period of study.

Scripture Affirms Joseph Smith's Mission

When I embarked on that assignment, I did not expect an in-depth study of the Savior's life to deepen my testimony of Joseph Smith's mission. But it did! The revelations recorded by Joseph Smith and insights found in the Bible are amazingly consistent.

Joseph Smith translated the Book of Mormon so quickly that he could not possibly have had time to cross-reference every verse that correlated with the Bible. So not only did my intense, six-week immersion in the scriptures expand my testimony of Jesus Christ; it reaffirmed my conviction that Joseph Smith was a prophet of God who translated the Book of Mormon by "the gift and power of God."[2]

You may be thinking that there is no way you would ever have enough time to undergo such a study. I wasn't sure where I would find the time either. I completed a major portion of it during the Christmas holiday break when my schedule was more flexible. Reading all of these verses in a relatively short period of time helped me see patterns that are more difficult to detect when studying just a few chapters or verses a day.

As I completed this exercise, I tried to imagine what it will be like, in a coming day, to present ourselves before the Savior. I feel certain we will be overwhelmed to the point of tears to be in His holy presence. We will struggle to find words to thank Him for paying for our sins, for forgiving us of our sins, and for healing us from the injustices and injuries of this life.

However, we do not have to wait until that day to understand more deeply the Savior's life, mission, and infinite Atonement. We can choose to increase our study of His words right now. As we do so, we will become one of His truly converted disciples, and our ability to be more like Him will increase.

The Book of Mormon Is a Miracle

Because of its power to teach truth, let us focus on the miracle that is the Book of Mormon!

The Book of Mormon is part of a remarkable prophecy recorded by Isaiah, speaking for the Lord: "I will proceed to do a marvellous work among this people, even a marvellous work and a wonder."[3]

The words *marvellous* and *wonder* were both translated from Hebrew terms meaning "extraordinary," "difficult to understand," or "miraculous."[4] Thus, the phrase "a marvellous work and a wonder" could also be translated as "a miraculous miracle." The coming forth of the Book of Mormon is indeed "a miraculous miracle."

With Oliver Cowdery as principal scribe, Joseph began translating on Tuesday, April 7, 1829,[5] and finished some seventy to eighty-five days later. Of course, not all of Joseph's and Oliver's time was spent working on the translation. During this period, Joseph also received the Aaronic and Melchizedek Priesthoods, received and recorded twelve revelations that are now sections of the Doctrine and Covenants,[6] moved from one state to another, applied for a copyright, and began making arrangements for the publication of the Book of Mormon. Conservatively estimated, some sixty-five or fewer working days would have been left for the work of translation. The 1830 edition contained 588 pages.[7] Thus, Joseph translated at the rate of about nine pages per day. Many of us consider it a major feat if we *read* nine pages of the Book of Mormon a day!

Oliver Cowdery later testified: "These were days never to be forgotten—to sit under the sound of a voice dictated by the inspiration of heaven, awakened the utmost gratitude of this bosom! Day after day I continued, uninterrupted, to write from his mouth, as he translated . . . the history or record called 'The Book of Mormon.'"[8]

Emma Smith, who acted as an earlier scribe for Joseph, gave this account: "When my husband was translating the Book of Mormon, I wrote part of it, as he dictated each sentence, word for word, and when he came to proper names he could not pronounce, or long words, he spelled them out, and while I was writing them, if I made a mistake in spelling, he would stop me and correct my spelling, although it was impossible for him to see how I was writing them down at the time. Even the word *Sarah* he could not pronounce at first, but had to spell it, and I would pronounce it for him.

"When he stopped for any purpose at any time he would, when he commenced again, begin where he left off without any hesitation."[9]

On another occasion, Emma recalled: "Joseph Smith . . . could neither write nor dictate a coherent and well-worded letter; let alone dictating a book like the Book of Mormon. . . . I was an active participant in the scenes that transpired . . . it is marvelous to me, 'a marvel and a wonder.'"[10]

The Power of the Book of Mormon

The value and power of the Book of Mormon lies not in the miracle of its translation, astonishing as it was. Its great worth is as another testament of Jesus Christ. Its four major authors and compilers—Nephi, Jacob, Mormon, and Moroni—were all eyewitnesses of the Lord, as was Joseph, the inspired translator of that book.

During one period of studying the Book of Mormon, I found myself making lists of what the Book of Mormon *is*, what it *affirms*, what it *refutes*, what it *fulfills*, what it *clarifies*, and what it *reveals*. Looking at the Book of Mormon through these lenses was insightful and inspiring! I recommend this exercise to all who want to plumb its depths more completely.

Regardless of the way you study this precious book, immersing yourself regularly in the truths of the Book of Mormon can be life-changing because it contains the answers to life's most compelling questions.

The Book of Mormon is the great clarifier of doctrine. It refutes many myths, affirms profound truths, and exposes the tactics of the adversary.[11]

The Book of Mormon refutes the concept of predestination. It refutes the idea of the creation *ex nihilo*—"out of nothing." It refutes the false notion of original sin, the practice of infant baptism, and the notion that revelation ended with the Bible. It refutes the adequacy of individual goodness alone without exalting ordinances for exaltation.

On the other hand, the Book of Mormon affirms the existence of a living and loving Father in Heaven. It affirms the nature of our

Heavenly Father's plan of salvation, happiness, and mercy. It declares the divinity of Jesus Christ.

The Book of Mormon stands as a global beacon of eternal truth. About this book the Lord said: "The testimony of two nations is a witness unto you that I am God, that I remember one nation like unto another? Wherefore, I speak the same words unto one nation like unto another. And when the two nations shall run together the testimony of the two nations shall run together also."[12]

The Book of Mormon affirms the supreme status of man's moral agency and sets forth eternal standards of accountability for our choices. It affirms the reality and inevitability of our impending judgment, which will be done with a perfect blending of the justice and mercy of God.[13] The Book of Mormon reveals that the keeper of the gate at Judgment will be Jesus, the Holy One of Israel. Each one of us will stand before Him to be judged.[14]

The Book of Mormon affirms the reality of premortal life and the sanctity of the sacrament. It reveals the state of the soul between death and resurrection, the endless nature of the priesthood of God, and the foreordination of choice spirits called and prepared from the foundation of the world for leadership in these latter days. From the Book of Mormon, we know that each one of us has been reserved to come forth at this particular time to accomplish the work we have been called to do.

The Book of Mormon reveals the important interrelationships between the Creation, the Fall, and the Atonement. It reveals that Joseph, who was sold into Egypt, foresaw the Prophet Joseph Smith and his day and noted that there would be many similarities in their lives.[15] Centuries later, the Prophet Joseph stated, "I feel like Joseph in Egypt."[16]

The Book of Mormon reveals that the inheritance of Joseph, son of Israel, was not forgotten when land was distributed to the tribes of Israel, as promised in the Abrahamic covenant. Joseph's inheritance was to be a land choice above all others.[17] It was choice because it was chosen to be the repository of sacred writings on golden plates from which the Book of Mormon would one day come. It was choice because it would eventually house the world headquarters of the restored Church of Jesus Christ in the latter days. And it was choice because it is a land of liberty for those who worship the Lord and keep His commandments.[18]

The Book of Mormon teaches what it really means to be born again. From it we learn about the gathering of scattered Israel. We know why we are here on earth. We learn how to contend with the adversary's deceptions. These and other truths like them are more powerfully and persuasively taught in the Book of Mormon than in any other book of scripture.

Most importantly, the Book of Mormon reveals that Jesus of Nazareth is literally the Son of God. No book of scripture bears more solemnly the weighty burden of that testimony than does the Book of Mormon.

The Book of Mormon teaches of the Atonement of Jesus Christ. The word *atone* in any of its forms appears in the King James translation of the New Testament only once.[19] In the Book of Mormon, *atone* in any of its forms appears thirty-nine times![20] No wonder this book contains the *fullness* of the gospel. It elucidates the Atonement of Jesus Christ!

The power of the Book of Mormon is most evident in the mighty change that comes into the lives of those who read it "with a sincere heart, with real intent, having faith in Christ."[21] It is no wonder that the Prophet Joseph Smith called the Book of Mormon "the most correct of any book on earth, and the keystone of our religion" and then promised that "a man would get nearer to God by abiding by its precepts, than by any other book."[22]

The coming forth of the Book of Mormon is the prophesied sign that "the Lord has commenced to gather Israel and fulfill His covenants."[23] And, the Book of Mormon is the instrument by which the promised gathering of Israel is being, and will be, accomplished, because it leads the sincere in heart to a testimony of Jesus Christ and His restored gospel.

The Book of Mormon Touches Hearts

In 1986, I was invited to give a special lecture at a university in Accra, Ghana. There I met a number of dignitaries, including an African tribal king. As we visited prior to the lecture, the king spoke to me only through his linguist.

After my lecture, the king made his way directly to me, but this time without his linguist. To my surprise, he spoke in perfect English—the Queen's English, I might add!

The king seemed puzzled. "Just who are you?" he asked.

"I am an ordained Apostle of Jesus Christ," I replied.

"What can you teach me about Jesus Christ?" the king asked.

I responded with a question: "May I ask what you already know about Him?"

The king's response revealed he was a serious student of the Bible and one who loved the Lord.

I then asked if he knew about the ministry of Jesus Christ to the people of ancient America. He did not. I explained that after the Savior's Crucifixion and Resurrection, He came to the people of ancient America and taught them His gospel.

"That record," I continued, "is what we know as the Book of Mormon. It is another testament of Jesus Christ. It is a companion scripture to the Holy Bible."

At this point, the king became *very* interested. I then opened a copy of the Book of Mormon to 3 Nephi chapter 11, and together the king and I read the Savior's sermon to the Nephites. I then presented the copy of the Book of Mormon to him. His response was priceless: "You could have given me diamonds or rubies, but nothing is more precious to me than this additional knowledge about the Lord Jesus Christ."

After experiencing the power of the Savior's words in 3 Nephi, the king proclaimed, "If I am converted and join the Church, I will bring my whole tribe with me."

"Oh, King," I said, "it doesn't work that way. Conversion is an individual matter. The Savior ministered to the Nephites one by one. Each individual receives a witness and testimony of the gospel of Jesus Christ for himself or herself."[24]

Something powerful happens when a child of God seeks to know more about Him and His Beloved Son. Nowhere are those truths taught more clearly and powerfully than in the Book of Mormon.

When I think of the Book of Mormon, I think of the word *power*. The truths of the Book of Mormon have the *power* to heal, comfort, restore, succor, strengthen, console, teach, inform, enlighten, and cheer our souls.

I promise that as you prayerfully study the Book of Mormon *every day*, you will make better decisions—*every day*. I promise that as you ponder what you study, the windows of heaven will open, and you will receive answers to your own questions and direction for your own life. I promise that as you daily immerse yourself in the Book of Mormon, you can be immunized against the evils of our day.

Whenever I hear anyone say, "I know the Book of Mormon is true," I want to exclaim, "That's nice, but it is not enough!" We need to feel, deep in "the inmost part" of our hearts,[25] that the Book of Mormon is unequivocally the word of God. We must feel it so deeply that we would never want to live even one day without it.

One of the most profound truths I have learned during a hundred years of living is that the Book of Mormon has the power to change our hearts and help us overcome the natural man. The Book of Mormon *is* the book that will help to prepare the world for the Second Coming of the Lord Jesus Christ—because it will help prepare a people ready to receive Him.

CHAPTER 14

LEARN TO RECEIVE PERSONAL REVELATION

This spiritual gift opens heaven's door to countless other gifts.

After my wife Dantzel died, I was not sure how to proceed. I found myself grappling with the question of whether I should remarry.

I sought the counsel of President Gordon B. Hinckley. He did not tell me what to do. He only acknowledged that if I did not remarry, there might be some assignments that would be difficult to give to me. This was in the back of my mind when a series of circumstances brought Wendy Watson, then a professor of marriage and family therapy at BYU, to my attention. I felt an unmistakable prompting of the Spirit to get acquainted with her, and several months later, I asked her to marry me. I still remember saying to her at that important moment, "I don't know you very well yet, but I do know revelation and how to receive it." To her credit—and as I came to learn is typical of her—she had already sought and received her own revelation about us, which gave her the courage to say yes!

I had been learning to interpret the whisperings of the Spirit for decades prior to this important episode in my life. Some of those learnings took place in the operating room.

One of the more dramatic learning experiences with the Spirit happened early in my surgical career when Brother E. Lyman, a stake patriarch living in southern Utah, sought my help. He had two critical issues with his heart: mitral stenosis and tricuspid valve regurgitation. In other words, this man had two faulty valves—one that could be repaired surgically and one that could not. So, I declined to operate.

Brother Lyman left that day disappointed, but he returned later to ask if I would reconsider. Again, I declined. When Brother Lyman returned a third time, he was not going to take no for an answer. With emotion, he said, "Dr. Nelson, I have prayed for help and have been directed to you. The Lord will not reveal to me how to repair both of my valves, but He can reveal it to you. If you will operate on me, the Lord will make it known to you what to do. Please perform the operation that I need, and please pray for the help that you need."

This was in 1960. To that point, I had performed a sum total of seventy-three open-heart operations. At the time, this seemed significant, but by today's standards, it would not be. Cardiothoracic surgeons today complete several hundred operations by the time they finish their residency. Further, I had performed only eight open-field operations on the mitral valve, the closest surgical equivalent to the tricuspid valve, and I had performed only two repairs for mitral valve insufficiency. Most significantly, at that time, no one knew how to repair a leaking tricuspid valve.

Brother Lyman's great faith influenced me. I could not bring myself to turn him away a third time, and I agreed to operate. I set the date of the operation for May 24, 1960, and began to pray to know what to do. Prior to the operation I received absolutely no impressions. As I entered the surgical suite to open Brother Lyman's chest, my resident, Dr. Maunsel B. Pearce, looked at me and said, "What are you going to do for his tricuspid regurgitation?"

I responded simply, "I have no idea."

We commenced the operation and first cleared the obstruction in the reparable valve. Then we exposed the second valve and found it to be intact and the tissue good. Its only problem was that it was extremely dilated. I could put my whole hand in Brother Lyman's tricuspid valve orifice instead of three fingers, which is the size it should have been.

It was while I was examining this valve that I had a clear impression: "*Reduce the circumference of the ring.*" My immediate thought was that I didn't know how to do that. Reducing the circumference of the ring was the equivalent of tightening the belt on a loose pair of pants. But you can't put a belt around the heart!

Then a diagram appeared in my mind showing me where to place sutures to do a series of tucks and pleats. This would reduce the circumference so that the valve tissue would cover the hole. It was, in essence, like cinching up the belt on a pair of loose trousers.

I can still vividly picture that mental image, complete with dotted lines where the sutures should be placed. I completed the repair on the tricuspid valve according to the diagram in my mind. As we finished the procedure and tested the valve, Dr. Pearce said, "It's a miracle."

I responded, simply, "It is an answer to prayer." I knew exactly from Whom the help had come.

I had never experienced such vivid revelation like that before, at least not surgically. Revelation enlightened my mind as I stood in the operating room that day. It was revelation, plain and simple. Revelation that not only saved that dear, faith-filled patriarch's life, but that gave instructions for other surgeons who could now help their patients with similar maladies.

When Amulek admonished his people to "cry unto him over the crops of your fields, that ye may prosper in them" and to "pour out your souls in your closets, and your secret places, and in your wilderness,"[1] he wasn't suggesting this just as a rote practice. He was teaching his people how to receive revelation. Prayer opens the door to revelation. Amulek was also teaching that revelation has no boundaries. As we learn to hear the voice of the Lord, He will direct us through the whisperings of the Spirit in all aspects of our lives. Nothing is off-limits.

The Lord Guides His Church through Revelation

The rest of my life has been blessed through the experience with revelation in the operating room that day with Brother Lyman's heart in my hands.

Ponder the miracle of it! We can pray to our Heavenly Father, in the name of Jesus Christ, and receive His guidance and direction; be warned about dangers and distractions; and be enabled to accomplish things we simply could not do on our own. If we will truly *receive* the gift of the Holy Ghost and learn to discern and understand His promptings, which are messages from God, we will be guided in matters large and small.

In January 2018, as I faced the daunting task of choosing two counselors to serve at my side in the First Presidency, I wondered how I could possibly choose just two from among the Apostles with whom I had served. I loved and cherished each one.

Because good inspiration is based upon good information, I prayerfully met one-on-one with each Apostle.[2] I then sequestered myself in a private room in the temple and sought the Lord's will.

The Lord was merciful and made His will abundantly clear. I should select President Dallin H. Oaks and President Henry B. Eyring to serve as my counselors in the First Presidency. In like manner, the Lord directed me to extend an apostolic call to Elders Gerrit W. Gong and Ulisses Soares.

No member of the First Presidency or Quorum of the Twelve Apostles would ever leave decisions for the Lord's Church to his own best judgment! When we convene as a Council of the First Presidency and Quorum of the Twelve, our meeting rooms become rooms of revelation. The Spirit is palpably present. As we wrestle with complex matters, a thrilling process unfolds. Each Apostle freely expresses his thoughts and point of view. Though we may differ initially in our perspectives, the love we feel for each other is constant. Our unity helps us work through differences of perspective and discern the Lord's will for His Church.

In our meetings, the majority *never* rules! We listen prayerfully to one another and talk with each other until we are united. When we reach complete accord, the unifying influence of the Holy Ghost is spine-tingling! We experience what the Prophet Joseph Smith taught, that "by union of feeling we obtain power with God."[3]

We May Each Receive Personal Revelation

The pattern of revelation we rely on at Church Headquarters is available to each seeking, searching man and woman, young adult, youth, and child who desires personal revelation for his or her own life. If Joseph Smith's transcendent experience in the Sacred Grove teaches us anything, it is that the heavens are open today and that God speaks to His children.

The Prophet Joseph Smith set a pattern for us to follow. Drawn to the promise of James that if we lack wisdom we may ask of God,[4] the young Joseph took his question directly to Heavenly Father. He sought personal revelation, and his seeking opened this last dispensation, the dispensation of the fullness of times.

In like manner, what will your seeking open for *you*? What wisdom do you lack? What do you feel an urgent need to understand? Find a quiet place where you can regularly go. Humble yourself and pour out your heart to your Heavenly Father. Turn to Him for answers and for comfort.

Pray in the name of Jesus Christ about your concerns, your fears, your weaknesses—yes, the very longings of your heart. And then listen! Record your thoughts and feelings. Realize that answers will not always be immediate. But as impressions come, follow through with the actions you are prompted to take. As you repeat this process day after day, month after month, year after year, you will "grow into the principle of revelation."[5]

Does God really want to speak to you? Yes! "As well might man stretch forth his puny arm to stop the Missouri river in its decreed course . . . as to hinder the Almighty from pouring down knowledge from heaven upon the heads of the Latter-day Saints."[6]

You do not have to wonder about what is true! "By the power of the Holy Ghost [we] may know the truth of all things."[7] You do not have to wonder whom you can safely trust. Through personal revelation, you can receive your own witness that the Book of Mormon is the word of God, that Joseph Smith is a prophet, and that this is the Lord's restored Church, with Jesus Christ Himself as the Head. Regardless of what others may say or do, no one can ever take away a witness that is borne to your heart and mind by the Holy Ghost about what is true.

I urge you to increase your capacity to receive revelation. The Lord has promised that "if thou shalt [seek], thou shalt receive revelation upon revelation, knowledge upon knowledge, that thou mayest know the mysteries and peaceable things—that which bringeth joy, that which bringeth life eternal."[8] Now *that* is a promise worth working and praying for!

No matter where you are on the covenant path, there is so much more that your Father in Heaven wants you to know. As Elder Neal A. Maxwell taught, "To those who have eyes to see and ears to hear, it is clear that the Father and the Son are giving away the secrets of the universe!"[9]

Nothing opens the heavens quite like the combination of increased purity, exact obedience, earnest seeking, regular time in temple and family history work, and daily feasting on the words of Christ in the Book of Mormon. For "the words of Christ will tell you all things what ye should do."[10]

To be sure, there will be times when you feel as though the heavens are closed. But as you continue to be obedient and honor the Lord's timetable, you will be given the knowledge you seek. Every blessing the Lord has for you—including miracles—will follow.

I am optimistic about the future. But I am also not naive about the days ahead. If we are to have any hope of sifting through the myriad of voices and the philosophies of men that attack truth, we must learn to receive personal revelation.

The Lord Wants Us to "Hear Him"

The adversary is clever. For millennia he has been making that which is good look evil and evil look good.[11] His messages tend to be loud, bold, and boastful.

Messages from our Heavenly Father, however, are strikingly different. He communicates simply, quietly, and with such stunning plainness that we cannot misunderstand Him.[12]

For example, whenever He has introduced His Only Begotten

Son to mortals upon the earth, He has done so with remarkably few words. On the Mount of Transfiguration to Peter, James, and John, God said, "This is my beloved Son: hear him."[13] His words to the Nephites in ancient Bountiful were, "Behold my Beloved Son, in whom I am well pleased, in whom I have glorified my name—hear ye him."[14] And to Joseph Smith, in the declaration that opened this dispensation, God simply said, "This is My Beloved Son. Hear Him!"[15]

Interestingly, in these three instances, just before the Father introduced the Son, the people involved were in a state of fear.

The Apostles were afraid when they saw Jesus Christ encircled by a cloud on the Mount of Transfiguration.

The Nephites were afraid because they had been through destruction and darkness for several days.

Joseph Smith was in the grips of a force of darkness just before the heavens opened.

However, when we seek to hear—truly hear—His Son, our Heavenly Father, through the promptings of the Holy Ghost, will guide us. We will know what to do in any circumstance and our fears will fall away.

Listen with the Intent to Obey

The very first word in the Doctrine and Covenants is *hearken*.[16] In the Old Testament, the word *hearken* is translated from the Hebrew *shama*, which is a strong verb that means to "listen with the intent to obey."

Thus, to hearken means to "hear Him"—to *hear* what the Savior says and then to *heed* His counsel. In those two words—"Hear Him"—God gives us the pattern for success, happiness, and joy in this life. We are to seek to *hear* the words of the Lord, *hearken* to them, and *heed* what He has told us!

As we seek to be true disciples of Jesus Christ, our efforts to *hear Him* need to be ever more intentional. It takes conscious and consistent effort to fill our daily lives with His words, His teachings, His truths.

What can we do so we can hear Him?

1. We can go to the scriptures. Daily immersion in the word of God prepares our minds and hearts to receive revelation.
2. We can go to the temple. The house of the Lord is a house of learning where the Lord teaches us in His own way. There we learn how to part the veil and communicate more clearly with heaven. There we learn how to rebuke the adversary and draw upon the Lord's priesthood power to strengthen us and those we love.
3. We can refine our ability to recognize the whisperings of the Holy Ghost. It has never been more imperative to learn how the Spirit speaks to you than right now.
4. We can heed the words of prophets, seers, and revelators. Ordained Apostles of Jesus Christ always testify of Him. They point the way as we make our way through the maze of mortality.

Increase Your Spiritual Capacity

Our Savior and Redeemer, Jesus Christ, will perform some of His mightiest works between now and when He comes again. We will see miraculous manifestations that God the Father and His Son, Jesus Christ, preside over this Church in majesty and glory.

However, in coming days, it will not be possible to survive spiritually without the guiding, directing, comforting, and constant influence of the Holy Ghost. So, I plead with you to increase your spiritual capacity to receive personal revelation. Choose to do the spiritual work required to experience the whisperings of the Holy Ghost. Choose also to hear the words of the Lord through scripture and through the words of prophets.

As you seek to more clearly receive direction from heaven, you will be blessed with additional power to deal with temptation, struggles, and weakness. I promise miracles in your marriage, family relationships, and daily work. And I promise that your capacity to feel joy will increase.

My beloved brothers and sisters, I plead with you to increase your capacity to receive revelation!

CHAPTER 15

MAKE THE TEMPLE YOUR SPIRITUAL FOUNDATION

Seek to know more, understand more, and feel more about temples.

I well remember when the Lord let the First Presidency know that it was time to renovate the Salt Lake Temple. This iconic structure needed extensive repairs to make the temple seismically safe and to address the wear and tear that had developed from more than a century of use.

It was clear that this would be a renovation project unlike any the Church had previously completed. There were those who suggested that such drastic measures need not be taken. The question of whether we should undertake such an ambitious effort weighed heavily upon me and my counselors. After consulting with many experts, and after counseling together as a First Presidency and seeking the Lord's guidance in prayer, we knew it was the Lord's will that we proceed.

It was, ironically, just a few weeks after we launched this massive project that the Salt Lake Valley was hit with a 5.8 magnitude earthquake—one strong enough to knock the trumpet off the Angel Moroni sitting atop the temple. That earthquake underscored the urgency of the project that was underway. Engineers told us that if the quake had been much larger, the stability of the entire temple would have been threatened.

After the first year of reconstruction, I had the opportunity to tour the construction site to better understand the components of this massive project. Looking at the original foundation of the Salt Lake Temple only enhanced my admiration for the efforts of President Brigham Young and his colleagues to build this magnificent structure in the late nineteenth century. As I examined their craftsmanship, I marveled at what the pioneers accomplished. When I considered that they built this magnificent edifice with only the crudest of tools, I was simply in awe.

Today, more than a century after the completion of the temple in 1893, as we examine the foundation closely, we can see the effects of erosion, gaps in the original stonework, and varying stages of stability in the masonry. As I witnessed firsthand what modern engineers are doing to reinforce the original foundation, I was amazed. Their work is mind-boggling!

The foundation of any building, particularly one as large as the Salt Lake Temple, must be strong and resilient enough to withstand earthquakes, corrosion, high winds, and the inevitable settling that affects all buildings. As a point of fact, I was interested to read not long ago about a fifty-eight-story condominium building in San Francisco that is sinking despite a costly plan to reinforce its foundation.[1] The complex task of strengthening the Salt Lake Temple's foundation will enable it to avoid any such catastrophe.

We are sparing no effort to give this house of the Lord a foundation that will withstand the forces of nature into the Millennium.

The Temple Forms the Foundation of Our Faith

In like manner, it is time that we each implement extraordinary measures—perhaps measures we have never taken before—to strengthen our personal spiritual foundations. Unprecedented times call for unprecedented measures.

We might ask ourselves, "How firm is *my* spiritual foundation?" What reinforcements to my testimony are needed to withstand the spiritual earthquakes in my life?"

The house of the Lord lies at the center of strengthening our faith and spiritual fortitude because the Savior and His doctrine are at the heart of the temple. Everything taught in the temple, through instruction and through the Spirit to those who are ready to learn, increases our understanding of Jesus Christ. His essential ordinances and the related covenants bind us to Him and to our Heavenly Father. Then, as we keep our covenants, He endows us with His healing, strengthening power. When we emerge from the temple, we do so armed with the Lord's power, with His glory round about us, and with His angels having charge over us.[2] And oh, how we will need His power, protection, and angels in the days ahead!

We have been promised that "if [we] are prepared [we] shall not fear."[3] Despite today's unprecedented challenges, those who build their foundation upon Jesus Christ need not succumb to the anxieties of this era.

The Apostle Paul prophesied that "in the last days perilous times [would] come."[4] And they surely have and will only increase. "For men shall be lovers of their own selves, covetous, boasters, proud, blasphemers, disobedient to parents, unthankful, unholy, without natural affection, trucebreakers, false accusers, incontinent, fierce, despisers of those that are good, traitors, heady, highminded, lovers of pleasures more than lovers of God."[5] One would almost think that Paul was reading the headlines of yesterday's news!

However, Paul also signaled great hope for our day. "We are troubled on every side, yet not distressed; we are perplexed, but not in despair,"[6] he said. This is particularly true for every covenant-making and covenant-keeping man and woman today.

Temple Ordinances Are Ancient

Adam and Eve, Abraham and Sarah, Noah and his wife, Lehi and Sariah, and all of God's faithful children through previous dispensations made the same covenants with God that we make with Him. To me, it is precisely the antiquity of these precious ordinances that provides important evidence of their authenticity.[7]

The Lord instructed Adam and Eve to pray, make covenants, and offer sacrifices. When an angel appeared to Adam and asked him why he made sacrifices to the Lord, Adam responded, "I know not, save the Lord commanded me."[8] Yet Adam and Eve were obedient to the Lord's commands and made sacrifices to Him.

It is no different for each of us. In the temple we covenant to live five laws: the laws of obedience, sacrifice, the gospel of Jesus Christ, chastity, and consecration. Each of these covenants requires a measure of sacrifice and submission to the Lord and His laws. Thus, "whenever the Lord has had a people on the earth who will obey His word, they have been commanded to build temples."[9] The standard works are replete with references to temple teachings, clothing, language, and more.

For example, the tabernacle of Moses was known as a "tent of the testimony"[10] and a "tabernacle of testimony."[11] Solomon's temple was destroyed in 587 BC, a few years after Lehi's family left Jerusalem. The restoration of this temple by Zerubbabel took place some seventy years later. It was then damaged by fire in 37 BC. Herod expanded the temple around 16 BC. Then this temple, which was known by Jesus, was destroyed by the Romans in AD 70. Further, Nephi had temple-like experiences by going "into the mount oft"[12] to pray, and later, in the Americas, built a temple "after the manner of the temple of Solomon."[13]

Everything we believe and *every* promise God has made to His covenant people comes together in the temple. In *every* age, the temple has underscored the precious truth that those who make covenants with God and keep them are children of the covenant.

Thus, in the house of the Lord, we can make the same covenants with God that Abraham, Isaac, and Jacob made. And we can receive the same blessings!

Temples Are Central to This Dispensation

Temples have been part of *this* dispensation from its earliest days. In 1833 the Lord told the Prophet Joseph Smith to "organize yourselves; prepare every needful thing; and establish a house, even a house of prayer, a house of fasting, a house of faith, a house of learning, a house of glory, a house of order, a house of God."[14]

Elijah committed the keys of sealing authority to Joseph Smith in the Kirtland Temple.[15] Then, the fullness of the priesthood was restored in the Nauvoo Temple, the cornerstone for which was laid on April 6, 1841, just a few months after Joseph Smith received the revelation to build it.

Until his martyrdom, Joseph Smith continued to receive revelations that furthered the restoration of the endowment and sealing ordinances. He recognized, however, that further refinement was needed. After administering the endowment to Brigham Young in May 1842, Joseph told Brigham, "This is not arranged right, but we have done the best we could under the circumstances in which we are placed, and I wish you to take this matter in hand and organize and systematize all these ceremonies."[16]

Following the Prophet's martyrdom, President Young oversaw the completion of the Nauvoo Temple. "Church Historian George A. Smith concluded that 5,634 brothers and sisters received their endowment in the partially completed Nauvoo Temple in December 1845 and January 1846. Sealings of couples continued on through Feb. 7, [1846,] by which time more than 2,000 couples had been united by the priesthood for time and eternity."[17]

President Young later built temples in the Utah Territory. At the dedication of the lower stories of the St. George Utah Temple, Brigham Young vigorously emphasized the urgency of vicarious temple work when he boldly declared, "What do you suppose the fathers would say if they could speak from the dead? Would they not say, 'We have lain here thousands of years, here in this prison house, waiting for this dispensation to come'? . . . Why, if they had the power the very thunders of heaven would be in our ears, if we could but realize the importance of the work we are engaged in. . . . When I think upon this subject, I want the tongues of seven thunders to wake up the people."[18]

Since that time, temple ordinances have been refined gradually. President Harold B. Lee explained why procedures, policies, and even the administration of temple ordinances continue to evolve: "The principles of the gospel of Jesus Christ are divine. Nobody changes the principles and [doctrine] of the Church except the Lord by revelation. But methods change as the inspired direction comes to those who preside at a given time."[19]

President Wilford Woodruff taught something similar when he declared, in 1896: "I want to say, as the president of the Church of Jesus Christ of Latter-day Saints, that we should now go on and progress. We have not [gotten] through with revelation. . . . President [Brigham] Young, who followed President Joseph Smith, led us here. He organized these temples and carried out the purposes of his calling and office. . . . He did not receive all the revelations that belong to this work; neither did President Taylor, nor has Wilford Woodruff. There will be no end to this work until it is perfected."[20]

As just one example, consider how administering the sacrament has changed over the years. In earlier days, the water of the sacrament was offered to the congregation in one large vessel from which everyone drank. Now we use individual disposable cups. The procedure changed, but the covenants remained the same.

The Restoration Is Ongoing

Please ponder these three significant truths:

First, the Restoration is a process, not an event, and will continue until Jesus Christ returns.

Second, the ultimate objective of the gathering of Israel[21] is to bring the blessings of the temple to God's faithful children.

Third, the ongoing Restoration needs ongoing revelation.

The First Presidency and Quorum of the Twelve Apostles have often asked God if there are better ways to take the blessings of the temple to His faithful children. We seek divine guidance regularly on how to ensure worldwide accuracy and consistency of temple instruction, covenants, and ordinances despite differences in languages and cultures.

In recent years, the Lord has authorized us to announce the building of temples in many new locations, some of them in remote areas. In answer to our prayers, the Lord has also authorized procedural adjustments to various temple ordinances. *He* is the One who wants you to understand exactly what you are making covenants to do. *He* is the One who wants you to comprehend your privileges, promises, and responsibilities. *He* is the One who wants you to have spiritual insights and awakenings you have never had before. He desires these for *all* temple patrons, no matter where they live.

Present adjustments in temple procedures, and others that will follow, are evidence that the Lord is actively directing His Church. These adjustments also signal how eager the Lord is for us to center our lives on Him and on the ordinances of His holy house. When you bring your temple recommend, a contrite heart, and a seeking mind to the Lord's house of learning, *He* will teach you.

Should distance, health challenges, or other constraints prohibit your temple attendance for a season, I invite you to set a regular time to rehearse in your mind the covenants you have made.

Go to the Temple More, Not Less

If you don't yet love to attend the temple, go more often—not less. Let the Lord, through His Spirit, teach and inspire you there. Over time, the temple will become a place of safety, solace, peace, instruction, revelation, and rejuvenation for you.

If it were possible for me to sit, knee-to-knee, with every young adult member of the Church, I would plead with you to seek a companion with whom you can be sealed in the temple. This crucial choice will make an extraordinary difference in your life. As you marry in the temple and return often, you will be guided in your decisions and your marriage will prosper.

If I could speak with each husband and wife who have still not been sealed in the temple, I would plead with you to take the necessary steps to receive that crowning, life-changing ordinance. Doing so will change not only your mortal lives but your eternal lives and those of your posterity.[22] No other ceremony or contract will make it so.[23]

If I could speak personally with each man or woman who longs for marriage but has not yet found his or her eternal companion, I would urge you to be endowed in the house of the Lord. Begin now to experience what it means to be armed with priesthood power. Seek now to understand what the temple can teach you about parting the veil, receiving revelation, and learning how to draw upon the precious privileges of the endowment.

To each of those who have made temple covenants, I plead with you to keep your covenants with ever-increasing precision. I plead with you to seek—prayerfully and consistently—to understand temple covenants and ordinances. Spiritual doors will open.

Elder John A. Widtsoe said it well: "The endowment is so richly symbolic that only a fool would attempt to describe it; it is so packed full of revelations to those who exercise their strength to seek and see, that no human words can explain or make clear the possibilities that reside in temple service. The endowment which was given by revelation can best be understood by revelation."[24]

Make the Temple Your Foundation

When renovations to strengthen the structural foundation of the Salt Lake Temple are completed, there will be *no safer place* during an earthquake in the entire Salt Lake Valley than inside that temple.

Likewise, whenever any kind of upheaval occurs in your life, the safest place to be *spiritually* is living *inside* your temple covenants.

Because the assaults of the adversary are increasing exponentially,[25] our need to be in the temple regularly has never been greater. If you have reasonable access to a temple, I urge you to find a way to make an appointment regularly with the Lord—to be in His holy house—and keep it. I promise you that the Lord will bring the miracles He knows you need as you make sacrifices to serve and worship in His temples.

The reward for keeping covenants with God is heavenly power. His power strengthens us to better withstand our trials, temptations, and heartaches. Those who live the higher laws of Jesus Christ have access to His higher power.

As you are true to your temple covenants, you will be strengthened by His power. Then, when spiritual earthquakes occur, you will be able to stand strong because your spiritual foundation is solid and immovable.

CHAPTER 16

EMBRACE THE CORRECT NAME OF THE CHURCH

The Lord honors those who reverence His name.

For as long as I have been at Church Headquarters, the question of using the correct name of the Church has been a recurring issue. Every time a department or Church organization wanted to use the word *Mormon* or the initials *LDS* in some way, this issue resurfaced. The ongoing debate about these "nicknames" invariably revolved around the belief by many that *Mormon* and *LDS* were simply too ingrained in the Church's lexicon to be discarded. The Church's main website was lds.org; the emails of Church leaders and employees ended with @lds.org. The list of other usages was long—The Mormon Tabernacle Choir, LDS Social Services, the "I'm a Mormon" campaign, Mormon.org, and the Mormon Channel being just a few examples.

Conventional wisdom declared that emphasizing the correct name of the Church simply wasn't doable—that the press would never go along with it, that in a digital age it was too late to effect such a massive change online, and that we as Church members were among the worst offenders.

It is true that the Church and its members have lived with nicknames such as *Mormon Church* and *Mormons* since the earliest days of the Restoration. Many of these terms originated as epithets designed to obliterate God's hand in restoring the Church of Jesus Christ. The word *Mormonites* was another term of derision that some opponents of the Church used.[1]

None of this changed the fact, however, that many of us at Headquarters knew this was a problem we needed to address.

In May of 2018, I took a short trip with President M. Russell Ballard, Acting President of the Quorum of the Twelve, and the two of us discussed the realities of this dilemma at length. After returning home and discussing this matter further with my counselors, we determined it was time to tackle the issue. I subsequently sent a letter to President Ballard, giving the Quorum of the Twelve the charge to resolve this dilemma.

On August 16, 2018, I issued the following statement: "The Lord has impressed upon my mind the importance of the name He has revealed for His Church, even The Church of Jesus Christ of Latter-day Saints. We have work before us to bring ourselves in harmony with His will. In recent weeks, various Church leaders and departments have initiated the necessary steps to do so. Additional information about this important matter will be made available in the coming months."[2]

Six weeks later, in the October 2018 general conference, I spoke to the members of the Church about the importance of using the correct name of the Church.

As expected, the responses to my press statement and general conference address were mixed. Many members immediately corrected the name of the Church on their blogs and social media pages.

Others wondered why I would focus so much attention on something so "inconsequential." Digital experts insisted that a correction at this point in time was unwise and would dramatically decrease the Church's visibility in the digital world. Others felt that because we as a people were so widely known as "Mormons" and as the "Mormon Church," the Church should make the best of it. Yet others said it was a fool's errand and could not be done, so why even try?

If this had been a discussion about branding a man-made organization, those arguments might have prevailed. But the Lord's ways are not man's ways. We felt confident that if we would be patient and do our part well, the Lord would lead us through this important task.

I am pleased to say that the Quorum of the Twelve Apostles, under President Ballard's superb leadership, handled this exceptionally difficult assignment with wisdom and inspiration. Within a year's time, we had corrected the names of the Church's websites, email addresses, social media pages, and many other entities—including correcting the name of the Mormon Tabernacle Choir to The Tabernacle Choir at Temple Square.

What's in a Name?

Why does the Lord care about this issue? Let me be clear about what this effort was *not*:

It was not a name change.

It was not rebranding.

It was not cosmetic.

It was not a whim.

And it absolutely was not inconsequential.

Instead, this was a *correction*. It was time to obey the command of the Lord, who said, "For thus shall my church be called in the last days, even The Church of Jesus Christ of Latter-day Saints."[3]

In AD 34, the resurrected Lord gave similar instruction to members of His Church in the Americas. At that time, He said: "Ye shall call the church in my name. . . . And how be it my church save it be called in my name? For if a church be called in Moses' name then it be Moses' church; or if it be called in the name of a man then it be the church of a man; but if it be called in my name then it is my church."[4]

Thus, the name of the Church is not negotiable. When the Savior declares what the name of His Church should be and even precedes His declaration with, "Thus shall my church be called," He is serious. If we allow nicknames to be used, and even sponsor those nicknames ourselves, He is offended.

What's in a name or, in this case, a nickname? When it comes to nicknames of the Church, such as the "LDS Church," the "Mormon Church," or the "Church of the Latter-day Saints," the most important thing in those names is the *absence* of the Savior's name. To remove the Lord's name from the Lord's Church is a victory for Satan. When we *discard* the Savior's name, we are openly disregarding all that Jesus Christ did for us—including His Atonement! When we ignore rather than reverence the Savior's name, we are ignoring Him.

Taking the Savior's Name upon Us

Jesus Christ chose to submit to the will of His Father and do something for all of God's children that no one else could do. Condescending to come to earth as the Only Begotten of the Father in the flesh, He was reviled, mocked, and scourged. In the Garden of Gethsemane, the Savior took upon Himself *every* pain, *every* sin, and all of the anguish and suffering ever experienced by *everyone* who has ever lived or will ever live. Under the weight of that excruciating burden, He bled from every pore[5] before being crucified on Calvary's cross.

Through these excruciating experiences and His subsequent Resurrection, Jesus Christ granted immortality to all and ransomed each one of us from the effects of sin on condition of our repentance.

After all the Savior of the world did for all of mankind, I realized with profound regret that we had unwittingly acquiesced in allowing the Lord's restored Church to be called by other names, each of which expunged the sacred name of Jesus Christ.

Every Sunday as we worthily partake of the sacrament, we make anew our sacred promise to our Heavenly Father that we are willing to take upon us the name of His Son, Jesus Christ.[6]

When we omit His name from His Church, we remove Him as the central focus of our worship and our lives.

Taking the Savior's name upon us includes declaring and witnessing to others—through our actions and our words—that Jesus is the Christ. Were we so afraid to offend those who called us "Mormons" that we failed to defend the Savior Himself, by not standing up for Him by not using the correct name of His Church?

If we as a people and as individuals are to have access to the power of the Atonement of Jesus Christ, we must clearly acknowledge Him as the source of that power. That begins with calling His Church by the name He decreed.

The Full Name Is a Long Name

We recognized that some individuals, including members of the media, would resist using the full name of the Church. We also hoped, however, that responsible media would be sympathetic to our request.

Elder Benjamin De Hoyos of the Seventy related such an event: "Some years ago while serving in the office of public affairs of the Church in Mexico, [a companion and I] were invited to participate in a radio talk show. . . . [One of the program directors] asked [us], 'Why does the Church have such a long name? . . .' My companion and I smiled at such a magnificent question and then proceeded to explain that the name of the Church was not chosen by man. It was given by the Savior. . . . The program director immediately and respectfully responded, 'We will thus repeat it with great pleasure.'"[7]

Sadly, but predictably, some have not yet respected our request to use the full name of the Church, though many have. We feel confident that, little by little, our best efforts will help correct errors that have crept in through the years. While we have no control over what other people call us, we are in complete control over how we refer to ourselves. The rest of the world may or may not follow our lead. However, we will honor the Lord's request to call His Church by His name!

What about the Word *Saint*?

I smile every time I remember a comment made after my call to the Quorum of the Twelve Apostles. A doctor friend relayed a report made at a professional meeting that "Dr. Nelson was no longer practicing cardiac surgery because his church had made him 'a saint.'"

That comment was not only amusing but revealing. It demonstrated unfamiliarity with the language of the Bible, in which the word *saint* is used much more frequently than is the word *Christian*. Despite its use in ninety-eight verses of the bible, the term *saint* is not well understood. Some mistakenly assume that it implies beatification or perfection. No! A saint is a person who believes in Jesus Christ and strives to follow Him.

If someone asks, "Are you a Latter-day *Saint*?" you might respond, "Yes, I am. I believe in Jesus Christ and am a member of His restored Church."

If someone asks, "Are you a Mormon?" you could reply, "If you are asking if I am a member of The Church of Jesus Christ of Latter-day Saints, yes, I am!"

Grand Blessings Await Us

When we announced our focus on restoring the correct name of the Church, I promised the members of the Church that if we would do our best, the Lord would pour down His power and blessings upon the heads of the Latter-day Saints.[8] I also promised that the Lord would help us take the blessings of the restored gospel of Jesus Christ to every nation, kindred, tongue, and people.

We are already seeing the fulfillment of these promises. Dignitaries, ambassadors, and religious leaders from around the globe—including from regions formerly hostile to the Church—are coming to Salt Lake City to meet with the First Presidency in unprecedented numbers. I believe many of our visitors would not be interested in meeting with the leaders of the "Mormon Church." However, they are seeking meetings with the leaders of the Church that bears the Lord's name.

We are a blessed people and have cause to rejoice.

So, what is in a name? When it comes to the name of the Lord's Church, the answer is, "Everything!" The Lord honors those who reverence His name and who call His Church by the correct name: The Church of Jesus Christ of Latter-day Saints.

CHAPTER 17

LET GOD PREVAIL IN OUR LIVES

You have a role in the greatest work on earth.

For the nearly forty years I have been an Apostle, the doctrine of the gathering of Israel has captured my attention. Many messages I have given reflect my fascination with and devotion to understanding what led to the dispersion of the tribes of Israel and what is required to gather them home in our day.

Everything about this topic has intrigued me, including the ministries and names of Abraham, Isaac, and Jacob; their lives and their wives; the covenant God made with them and extended through their lineage; the dispersion of the twelve tribes; and the numerous prophecies about the gathering in our day.

In Hebrew, *Abram* is a noble name meaning "exalted father." But when God changed Abram's name to *Abraham*, the name took on even greater significance, meaning "exalted father of a multitude." Indeed, Abraham was to be the "father of many nations."[1]

The covenant that Jehovah made with Abraham is a unique and

special one: that the Savior of the world would be born through Abraham's seed, that his posterity would receive certain lands, and that all nations would be blessed through Abraham's lineage.[2]

I have studied the gathering, prayed about it, feasted upon every related scripture again and again, and asked the Lord to increase my understanding.

So, imagine my delight when I was led just a few years ago to a new insight. With the help of two Hebrew scholars, I learned that one of the Hebraic meanings of the word *Israel* is "let God prevail." The very name of *Israel* refers to a person who is willing to let God prevail in his or her life. This concept stirs my soul!

The word *willing* is crucial to this interpretation of *Israel.* We all have our agency. We can choose to be of Israel, or not. We can choose to let God prevail in our lives, or not. We can choose to let God be the most powerful influence in our lives, or not.

The question for each of us is then, are we willing to let God prevail in our lives? Are we willing to let God be the most important influence in our lives? Will we allow His words, His commandments, and His covenants to influence what we do each day? Will we allow His voice to take priority over any other?

How Important Is the Gathering?

Let's take a moment to understand some important historical background. Jacob, the grandson of Abraham, faced a crucial turning point in his life. At the place Jacob named *Peniel,* which means "the face of God,"[3] Jacob wrestled with a serious challenge. His agency was tested. Through this wrestle, Jacob demonstrated that he was willing to let God prevail in his life. In response, God changed Jacob's name to *Israel,*[4] meaning "let God prevail." God then promised Israel that *all* the blessings that had been pronounced upon Abraham's head would also be his.[5]

Sadly, Israel's posterity broke their covenants with God, and He scattered them to the four corners of the earth.[6] Mercifully, God later promised to gather them, as reported by Isaiah: "For a small moment have I forsaken thee [Israel]; but with great mercies will I gather thee."[7]

With the Hebraic definition of *Israel* in mind, the gathering of Israel takes on added meaning. The Lord is gathering those who are *willing* to let God be the most important influence in their lives.

For centuries, prophets have foreseen and foretold the gathering[8] that is happening right now! As an essential prelude to the Second Coming of the Lord Jesus Christ, this gathering is *the most* important work in the world. As members of The Church of Jesus Christ of Latter-day Saints, or "latter-day covenant Israel,"[9] we have been charged to assist the Lord with this pivotal work.

Being a member of the house of Israel is not for the faint of heart. To receive the blessings that God promised Abraham's seed, we can each expect to have our own "Abrahamic test." God will test us, as the Prophet Joseph Smith taught, by wrenching our very heartstrings.[10]

Who Is Being Gathered?

The Lord has a wonderful way of describing those who are being gathered. He refers to us as His "peculiar treasure,"[11] His "jewels,"[12] and as a "holy nation."[13]

When we speak of gathering Israel on both sides of the veil, we are referring, of course, to missionary, temple, and family history work. We are also referring to building faith and testimony in the hearts of those with whom we live, work, and serve. Let me be clear about the magnitude of this work. *Anytime* we do *anything* that helps *anyone*—on either side of the veil—to make and keep their covenants with God, we are helping to gather Israel. It is as simple and as profound as that.

Not long ago, the wife of one of our grandsons was struggling spiritually. I will call her "Jill." Despite fasting, prayer, and priesthood blessings, Jill's father was dying. She was gripped with fear that she would lose both her dad and her testimony.

Late one evening, my wife Wendy told me about Jill's situation. The next morning, Wendy felt impressed to share with Jill that my response to her spiritual wrestle was one word! The word was *myopic*.

Jill later admitted that initially she was devastated by my response. She said, "I was hoping for Grandfather to promise me a miracle for my dad. I kept wondering why *myopic* was the word he felt compelled to say."

After Jill's father departed this world, the word *myopic* kept coming to her mind. At that point, she opened her heart and came to understand that *myopic* meant "nearsighted." That is when her thinking began to shift. "*Myopic* caused me to stop, think, and heal," Jill said. "That word now fills me with peace. It reminds me to expand my perspective and seek the eternal. It reminds me that there is a divine plan and that my dad still lives and loves and looks out for me. *Myopic* has led me to God."

I am so proud of Jill. During this heart-wrenching time in her life, she began to learn to embrace God's will for her father and keep an eternal perspective of her own. By *choosing* to let God prevail, Jill found peace.

There are many ways this Hebraic interpretation of *Israel* can help us. With this concept in mind, just imagine how our prayers for our missionaries—and for our own efforts in gathering Israel—could change. For example, we often pray that we and the missionaries will be led to those who are prepared to receive the truths of the restored gospel of Jesus Christ. I wonder if our efforts would be even *more* effective if we were to plead to *find those who are willing to let God prevail in their lives*?

We may be led to some who have never believed in God or Jesus Christ but who are now yearning to learn about Them and God's plan of happiness. Others to whom we may be led may have been "born in the covenant" but have since wandered away from the covenant path. The phrase "born in the covenant" refers to the covenant God made with Abraham, saying, "In thy seed shall all the kindreds of the earth be blessed."[14] The parents of those "born in the covenant" have been sealed in the temple.

Someone born in the covenant who has strayed from the covenant path may now be ready to repent, return, and to let God prevail in his or her life. We can help by welcoming them back with open arms and hearts. And some to whom we may be led may have always felt there was something missing in their lives but not known how to fill the gaps they felt.

The Gospel Net Is Expansive

There is room in the gospel net for every person who will embrace the gospel of Jesus Christ. Each convert becomes one of God's covenant children, whether by birth or by adoption. God explained this promise to Abraham: "As many as receive this Gospel shall be called after thy name, and shall be accounted thy seed, and shall rise up and bless thee, as their father."[15] Each person who is truly converted to Jesus Christ becomes a full heir to *all* that God has promised the faithful children of Israel!

One promise is that each faithful member may request a patriarchal blessing. Through the inspiration of the Holy Ghost, the patriarch declares that person's lineage in the house of Israel. That declaration is not necessarily a pronouncement of his or her race, nationality, or genetic makeup. Rather, the declared lineage identifies the tribe of Israel through which that person will receive his or her blessings.

Each of us has a divine potential because each is a child of God. Each of His faithful children is equal in His eyes. The implications of this truth are profound. God does not love one race more than another. His doctrine on this matter is clear. He invites *all* to come unto Him, "black and white, bond and free, male and female." For "all are alike unto God, both Jew and Gentile."[16]

I assure you that no one's standing before God is determined by the color of their skin. Favor or disfavor with God is dependent upon our devotion to Him and obedience to His commandments—not upon our nationality, language, gender, culture, or the color of our skin.

I grieve for all who have endured pains of racism and prejudice and renew a call upon our members to *lead out* in abandoning attitudes of prejudice. True followers of Jesus Christ are duty-bound to promote respect for all of God's children.

The question for each of us, regardless of race, nationality, gender, or sexual orientation, is the same. Are we willing to let God prevail in our lives? Are we willing to let God be the most important influence in our lives? And are we willing to be actively, intentionally engaged in gathering Israel? For gathering Israel is the greatest challenge, the greatest cause, and the greatest work on earth!

The Lord Is Hastening His Work

The Lord is hastening His work to gather Israel. Nothing else compares in magnitude, nothing else compares in importance, nothing else compares in majesty. Wendy had an experience that highlighted just how real the gathering is.

On June 15, 2013, we were in Moscow, Russia, to meet with the Saints there. While I met with priesthood leaders, Wendy met with about a hundred of our Russian sisters. As she began to speak, Wendy found herself saying something she had not anticipated. She asked the sisters to stand as she mentioned the tribe of Israel that represented the lineage declared in their patriarchal blessing.

As Wendy listed the names of the tribes of Israel—Benjamin, Dan, Reuben, Asher, Zebulun, and more—women stood. As she did so, she was amazed at what she was witnessing. In that small gathering of fewer than a hundred women, eleven of the twelve tribes of Israel were represented! Only the tribe of Levi was missing.

We then flew to Yerevan, Armenia, where the mission president and his wife met us as we arrived. Somehow, she had heard about Wendy's experience in Moscow, and with delight she greeted us with, "I've got Levi!" The next day we met an elder from Gilbert, Arizona, who was of the tribe of Levi. So, in less than twenty-four hours, Wendy had been in the presence of members of all twelve tribes of Israel!

Wendy later learned that, because patriarchal blessings are sacred and the lineage declared in them is personal, she should not have asked members to openly declare their lineage. But that experience demonstrated just how very real the gathering is.

When we speak of the gathering, we are simply saying this fundamental truth: that every one of Heavenly Father's children, on both sides of the veil, deserves to hear the message of the restored gospel of Jesus Christ and decide for themselves if they want to know more.

Those who will be identified from the various tribes of Israel are those whose hearts will most likely be turned to the Lord. He said, "My sheep hear my voice, and I know them, and they follow me."[17]

The gathering of scattered Israel in our day has profound significance, as the Lord told the Prophet Joseph: "For behold, the field is white already to harvest; and it is the eleventh hour, and the *last time* that I shall call laborers into my vineyard. . . . And even so will I gather mine elect from the four quarters of the earth, even as many as will believe in me, and hearken unto my voice."[18]

The question for each of us is, simply, Do we want to take part in the greatest challenge and the greatest cause on earth today? Do we want to be among the "swift messengers" of whom the prophet Isaiah spoke?[19]

Participating in the gathering of Israel will require some sacrifice on your part. It will take some of your time, energy, and God-given talent and spiritual gifts.

Every prophet commencing with Adam has seen our day and prophesied about how the world would prepare for the *Second Coming of the Savior*. Of all the people who have ever lived on planet earth, *we* are the ones who get to participate in this final, great gathering event. What could be more exciting than that?

What Can One Person Do?

Our Heavenly Father has reserved many of His most noble spirits—perhaps, I might say, His finest team—for this final phase. These noble spirits are you!

You may, however, be asking yourself, "What can I possibly do to help gather Israel?"

The answer is simple: Men and women, young men and young women, and even children become acquainted with the Church and its teachings one person at a time—often because they work or go to school or live next to Latter-day Saints with whom they become friends. They agree to listen to the missionaries one person at a time.

Conversion happens one person at a time and, very often, an introduction to The Church of Jesus Christ of Latter-day Saints takes place because one member chooses to live his or her covenants and exemplify how a disciple of Christ lives.

You can be the member who befriends a fellow student, colleague, or neighbor. You can demonstrate, by the way you live your life, what a faithful disciple of Jesus Christ looks and acts like. You can be one who builds bridges with others, shares a social post or copy of the Book of Mormon, or comes to the aid of someone in distress. You can be the Latter-day Saint who learns to speak comfortably about what you believe and why your beliefs make such a difference in your life.

You and I are living to see Israel gathered with real power. And *you* can be part of the power behind that gathering! To assist your efforts to join the gathering, I invite you to make a weekly sacrifice of time for the Lord. This might mean spending more time at the temple or doing family history research. It might mean carrying an extra copy of the Book of Mormon with you and striking up conversations about the Church as you commute to work. It might mean serving in a refugee center. And it certainly includes praying daily that all of God's children can receive the blessings of the gospel of Jesus Christ.

To the youth of the Church, I invite you to stand out. Be willing to be different from the world. "Let your light so shine before this people, that they may see your good works and glorify your Father who is in heaven."[20] The Lord needs you to look like, sound like, act like, and dress like a true disciple of Jesus Christ. He is counting on you to reflect His light in this ever-darkening world.

With the Holy Ghost as your companion, you can be smarter

than previous generations have been. And if you are ridiculed for your standards, you can wear that distinction as a badge of honor.

You are the hope of Israel, "children of the promised day."[21] Of this I am absolutely certain.

As you make sacrifices to participate in the Lord's soul-stretching work, you will literally save lives. That is why this is the greatest, most important work on earth!

CHAPTER 18

OVERCOME THE WORLD AND FIND REST

The reward for keeping covenants with God is heavenly power.

For decades I have kept an intense schedule. Medical school and the internships and residency that followed were rigorous. Research on the heart, setting up a surgical clinical practice, and teaching at various universities were invigorating as well as enervating. Treasured time with my wife and ten children, and serving in Church callings, stretched me further. There were many times when I was simply exhausted and longed for rest.

The life of a General Authority is not much different. Getting on and off airplanes, week after week—often during lengthy trips—is taxing. I often say to Wendy, "We don't believe in jet lag. We don't have time." Gratefully, the joy of being with the people offsets the weariness. However, I know how real fatigue feels.

One of the plagues of this era seems to be the tendency to squeeze as much activity into our lives as possible. Yet sleep is essential to allow our minds and bodies to recharge. Sleep helps our bodies stay healthy and ward off disease. Without enough sleep, our brains cannot function properly. A reasonable amount of rest is vital to overall health and well-being.

The Most Important Rest Is Spiritual Rest

There is another kind of rest that is equally vital. We are accosted almost daily by an onslaught of disturbing news. You may have had days when you wished you could don your pajamas, curl up in a ball, and ask someone to wake you when the turmoil is over.

On the other hand, so many wonderful things are ahead. In coming days, we will see the *greatest* manifestations of the Savior's power that the world has *ever* seen. Between now and the time the Lord returns "with power and great glory,"[1] He will bestow countless privileges, blessings, and miracles upon the faithful.

Nonetheless, we are presently living in what surely is one of the most complicated times in the history of the world. The complexities and challenges—not to mention animosities—leave many people feeling overwhelmed and exhausted. However, an experience that occurred during the open house of the renovated Washington D.C. Temple sheds light on how we can find rest.

A member of the open house committee witnessed an insightful interchange as he escorted several prominent journalists through the temple. Somehow a young family became attached to what was actually a media tour. One reporter kept asking about the "journey" of a temple patron as he or she moves through the temple. He wanted to know if the temple journey is symbolic of the challenges in a person's journey through life.

A young boy in the family picked up on the conversation. When the tour group entered an endowment room, the boy pointed to the altar, where people kneel to make covenants with God, and said,

"Oh, that's nice. Here is a place for people to *rest* on their temple journey."

The boy surely had no idea just how profound his observation was. He likely did not understand the direct connection between making a covenant with God in the temple and the Savior's stunning promise: "Come unto me, all ye that labour and are heavy laden, and I will give you *rest*. Take my yoke upon you, and learn of me; . . . and ye shall find *rest* unto your souls. For my yoke is easy, and my burden is light."[2]

As I contemplate these verses, which are so rich in meaning and comprise a fundamental promise from the Savior Himself, I grieve for those who leave the Church because they feel membership requires too much of them. They have not yet discovered that making and keeping covenants actually makes life easier! Each person who makes covenants in baptismal fonts and in temples—and keeps those covenants—has increased access to the power of Jesus Christ.

Living Higher Laws Leads to Higher Power

The reward for keeping covenants with God is heavenly power—power that strengthens us to better withstand our trials, temptations, and heartaches. This power eases our way. Those who live the higher laws of Jesus Christ have access to His higher power. Thus, covenant keepers are entitled to a special kind of *rest* that comes to them through their covenantal relationship with God.

Before the Savior submitted Himself to the agony of Gethsemane and Calvary, He declared to His Apostles, "In the world ye shall have tribulation: but be of good cheer; I have overcome the world."[3] Subsequently, Jesus entreated each of us to do the same when He said, "I will that *ye* should overcome the world."[4]

Imagine how different this world would be if everyone

understood this simple truth: that because Jesus Christ overcame this fallen world, and because He atoned for each of us, we too can overcome this sin-saturated, self-centered, and often exhausting world!

Because the Savior, through His infinite Atonement, redeemed each of us from weakness, mistakes, and sin, and because He experienced every pain, worry, and burden we will ever have,[5] as we truly repent and seek His help, our burdens will be lightened and we can rise above this present precarious world.

We can overcome the spiritually and emotionally exhausting plagues of the world, including arrogance, pride, anger, immorality, hatred, greed, jealousy, and fear. Despite the distractions and distortions that swirl around us, we can find true rest—meaning relief and peace—even amid our most vexing problems.

This important truth prompts three fundamental questions:

First, what does it mean to overcome the world?

Second, how do we do it?

And third, how does overcoming the world bless our lives?

What Does It Mean to Overcome the World?

Overcoming the world means overcoming the temptation to care more about the things of this world than the things of God. Because this is so important, let me say it another way: Overcoming the world means our focus is much more on the things of God than on the things of this world. It means trusting the doctrine of Christ more than the philosophies of men. Overcoming the world means delighting in truth, denouncing deception, and becoming "humble followers of Christ."[6] It means choosing to refrain from things that drive the Spirit away. It means being willing to "give away" all our sins, even our favorites.[7]

Overcoming the world certainly does not mean becoming

perfect in this life, nor does it mean that your problems will magically evaporate—because they will not. And it does *not* mean that you won't still make mistakes, because you will. But overcoming the world *does* mean that your resistance to sin will increase and your heart will soften as your faith in Jesus Christ increases.

The Book of Mormon prophet King Benjamin spelled out this process for his people when he taught them that "because of the covenant which ye have made ye shall be called the children of Christ, his sons, and his daughters; for behold, this day he hath spiritually begotten you; for ye say that your hearts are changed through faith on his name; therefore, ye are born of him and have become his sons and his daughters."[8]

In short, overcoming the world means growing to love God and His Beloved Son more that you love anyone or anything else! It means developing a soft heart that is receptive to the promptings of the Holy Ghost—a heart that desires to do whatever the Lord would have you do.

How, then, do we overcome the world? King Benjamin taught us how. He said that "the natural man is an enemy to God" and remains so forever "*unless* he yields to the enticings of the Holy Spirit, and putteth off the natural man and becometh a saint through the atonement of Christ the Lord."[9]

Each time we seek for and follow the promptings of the Spirit, each time we do anything good—things that the "natural man" would *not* do—we are overcoming the world.

Overcoming the world is not an event that happens in a day or two. It happens over a lifetime as we repeatedly embrace the doctrine of Christ. We cultivate faith in Jesus Christ by repenting daily and keeping covenants that endow us with power. We stay on the covenant path and are blessed with spiritual strength, personal revelation, increasing faith, a greater desire to repent daily, and the ministering of angels. Living the doctrine of Christ will produce a powerful virtuous cycle, creating spiritual momentum in our lives.[10] Living the doctrine of Christ softens our hearts!

This is because as we strive to live the higher laws of Jesus Christ, first our hearts and then our very natures begin to change. The Savior *lifts* us above the pull of this fallen world by blessing us with greater charity, humility, generosity, kindness, self-discipline, peace, and, yes, *rest.*

The Blessings of Overcoming the World

Now, this may sound more like hard spiritual work than *rest.* But here is the grand truth: while the world insists that power, possessions, popularity, and pleasures of the flesh bring happiness and joy, they do not. They cannot. What they do produce is a hollow, temporary substitute for "the blessed and happy state of those [who] keep the commandments of God."[11]

I have witnessed this again and again! The truth of the matter is that it is much *more exhausting* to seek happiness where you can *never* find it! On the other hand, when we yoke ourselves to Jesus Christ and do the spiritual work required to overcome the world, He has the power to lift us above the pull of this world and to give us rest.

How does overcoming the world bless our lives? The answer is clear: Entering into a covenant relationship with God binds us to Him in a way that makes *everything* about life easier. Please do not misunderstand me on this point: I did *not* say that making covenants makes life easy. In fact, expect opposition, because the adversary does not want us to discover the power of Jesus Christ or how willing He is to help us. But yoking ourselves to the Savior means we have access to *His* strength and enabling, healing, redeeming power.

I reaffirm a profound teaching of President Ezra Taft Benson: "Men and women who turn their lives over to God will discover that He can make a lot more out of their lives than they can. He will deepen their joys, expand their vision, quicken their minds, strengthen their muscles, lift their spirits, multiply their blessings, increase their opportunities, comfort their souls, raise up friends, and pour out peace. Whoever will lose his life in the service of God will find eternal life."[12]

These incomparable privileges follow those who seek the support of heaven to help them overcome this world.

To this end—with the quest to overcome the world clearly fixed in our hearts—I plead with each of us to take charge of our own testimonies of Jesus Christ and His gospel. This requires work. It takes nurturing. It takes regular searching, seeking, contemplation, and study. It means refusing to pollute our testimonies with the philosophies of unbelieving men and women.

I can assure anyone who accepts this challenge that as you make the continual strengthening of your testimony of Jesus Christ your *highest* priority, you will experience miracles in your life.

Honoring Covenants Leads to Rest

My plea to all is to find rest from the intensity, uncertainty, and anguish of this world by overcoming the world through our covenants with God. Let Him know through your prayers and your actions that you are serious about overcoming the world. Ask Him to enlighten your mind and send the help you need. Increase the time you serve and worship in the temple, if possible, because the temple teaches us how to rise above this fallen world. Indeed, President David O. McKay taught that the temple endowment is a "step-by-step ascent into the Eternal Presence."[13]

As I have stated previously, the gathering of Israel is the most important work taking place on earth today. One crucial element of this gathering is to prepare a people who are able, ready, worthy, and willing to receive the Lord when He comes again. This means a people who have already chosen Jesus Christ over this fallen world, a people who rejoice in their agency to live the higher, holier laws of Jesus Christ.

I call upon you, my dear friends, my dear brothers and sisters, to become this righteous people. Cherish and honor your covenants above all other commitments. As you allow God to prevail in your life, I promise you greater peace, confidence, joy, and *rest*.

With the power of the holy apostleship vested in me, I bless you in your quest to overcome this world. I bless you to increase your faith in Jesus Christ and learn better how to draw upon His power. I bless you to be able to discern truth from error. I bless you to care more about the things of God than the things of the world and to become a more devoted disciple of Jesus Christ. And I bless you to assist with the needs of those around you and to strengthen those you love.

Through the ups and downs, the joys and heartaches, of a century of living, there is nothing of which I am more certain than that Heavenly Father is *our* Father, that His Only Begotten Son, Jesus Christ, is *our* Savior and Redeemer, and that the Holy Ghost can be your constant companion, whispering truths to your soul. I am certain that the gospel of Jesus Christ has been restored in its fullness and is filled with the Savior's power to bless you in ways no one else and nothing else can.

I leave you with my assurance that because Jesus Christ overcame this world, you can too.

NOTES

Chapter 1: Begin with the End in Mind

1. Proverbs 29:18.
2. Moses 1:39.
3. John 6:38.
4. Mosiah 2:41.
5. See Sarah Jane Weaver, "We are going to start with the end in mind," thechurchnews.com, May 4, 2018.
6. Abraham 3:25–26.
7. Titus 1:2.
8. 2 Nephi 28:7.
9. See 2 Timothy 3:1–5.
10. See Doctrine and Covenants 45:26.
11. See 2 Timothy 3:2–4.
12. See Doctrine and Covenants 10:5.
13. Ephesians 6:12.
14. 2 Nephi 2:25.

15. Governor Lilburn W. Boggs of Missouri issued the order of extermination of all Latter-day Saints on October 27, 1838. See *Teachings of Presidents of the Church: Joseph Smith* (2007), 349.
16. See Eliza R. Snow in Edward W. Tullidge, *The Women of Mormondom* (1877), 145–46.
17. Philippians 4:7.
18. Doctrine and Covenants 121:7.
19. See 2 Nephi 2:2.
20. Hebrews 12:2.
21. Hebrews 12:2.
22. See Ether 12:27.
23. See Doctrine and Covenants 122:7.
24. See Matthew 19:26; Mark 10:27.
25. Alma 30:22; emphasis added.
26. 2 Nephi 9:18.
27. See 2 Nephi 27:30; Alma 27:16–18.

Chapter 2: Discover the Power of Divine Law

1. Doctrine and Covenants 88:36–38.
2. Doctrine and Covenants 130:21.
3. John 8:32.
4. *Teachings of Presidents of the Church: Joseph Smith* (2007), 210.
5. Spencer W. Kimball, "Absolute Truth" (Brigham Young University devotional, September 6, 1977), speeches.byu.edu.
6. Spencer W. Kimball, "Absolute Truth."
7. Jacob 4:13.
8. See Matthew 7:24–27.

Chapter 3: Understand the Everlasting Covenant

1. See Russell M. Nelson, "Children of the Covenant," *Ensign*, May 1995.
2. Moses 6:67–68.
3. A comprehensive discussion regarding *hesed* and the everlasting covenant is found in Kerry Muhlestein, *God Will Prevail: Ancient*

Covenants, Modern Blessings, and the Gathering of Israel (American Fork, UT: Covenant Communications, 2021).

4. Doctrine and Covenants 132:31.
5. Doctrine and Covenants 132:19.
6. Malachi 4:6.
7. Joseph Smith—History 1:39.
8. John 14:6.
9. See Genesis 11:29.
10. See Genesis 11:30; 16:1.
11. See Genesis 16:3.
12. See Genesis 16:11. The Hebrew term *Ishmael* means "God heareth."
13. See Hebrews 11:11: "Through faith also Sara herself received strength to conceive seed, and was delivered of a child when she was past age, because she judged him faithful who had promised."
14. See Genesis 17:19.
15. See Genesis 17:5, 15.
16. See Genesis 17:20.
17. See Genesis 17:19.
18. Galatians 3:27–29.
19. See Genesis 32:28.
20. Exodus 19:5.
21. Acts 3:13.
22. Acts 3:25.
23. 3 Nephi 20:25–26.
24. Helaman 3:27.
25. Doctrine and Covenants 110:15.
26. Doctrine and Covenants 110:12.
27. Russell M. Nelson, "Thanks for the Covenant" (Brigham Young University devotional, November 22, 1988), speeches.byu.edu.
28. See Deuteronomy 7:9.
29. "Every covenant with God is an opportunity to draw closer to him. To anyone who reflects for a moment on what they have already felt of the love of God, to have that bond made stronger and that relationship closer is an irresistible offer" (Henry B. Eyring, "Making Covenants

with God" [Brigham Young University devotional, September 8, 1996], speeches.byu.edu).

30. Doctrine and Covenants 14:7.
31. See Hebrews 7:22.
32. See Genesis 41:50–52; 46:20.
33. See Mormon 5:20; 9:37.
34. Russell M. Nelson, "The Future of the Church: Preparing the World for the Savior's Second Coming," *Ensign*, April 2020.

Chapter 4: Understand Who You Are and Whose You Are

1. Doctrine and Covenants 93:36.
2. See 1 Corinthians 15:22.
3. See John 11:25.
4. See 2 Nephi 9:41; Mormon 3:20.
5. See John 14:2; Joseph Smith Translation, 1 Corinthians 15:40; Doctrine and Covenants 76:89–98; 131:1.
6. Dallin H. Oaks, "Divine Love in the Father's Plan," *Liahona*, May 2022.
7. John 14:2.
8. Alma 34:32.
9. Doctrine and Covenants 76:111; emphasis added.
10. See Doctrine and Covenants 88:22–24.
11. Abraham 3:26.
12. 1 Corinthians 15:41; Doctrine and Covenants 76:96.
13. See Doctrine and Covenants 88:28–32.
14. Doctrine and Covenants 88:22.
15. 3 Nephi 20:25.
16. Acts 3:25.
17. *Hymns* (1985), no. 301.
18. See *General Handbook: Serving in The Church of Jesus Christ of Latter-day Saints*, 11.1.2; 10.1.2, ChurchofJesusChrist.org.
19. See Mosiah 18:8–10.
20. Adam died at age 930. Noah died at age 950. See Genesis 5:5; 9:29.
21. See 3 Nephi 7, for example.
22. See "Remarks," *Deseret News*, December 21, 1859, 322.

23. Romans 8:17.
24. See John 16:33; Doctrine and Covenants 50:41.
25. Alma 7:14.
26. See 1 Nephi 4:3.
27. See Luke 4:18; Alma 7:10–12.
28. Moses 1:39.
29. See Psalm 116:15.
30. Doctrine and Covenants 121:28.
31. See Luke 22:32.

Chapter 5: Reject the Plague of Contention

1. Matthew 5:9. The Savior's promise to peacemakers is that they will be "called the children of God."
2. Matthew 5:25.
3. Matthew 5:39.
4. Matthew 5:44.
5. See John 13:34.
6. John 13:35.
7. 3 Nephi 11:29.
8. 3 Nephi 13:24.
9. Articles of Faith 1:13.
10. See Moroni 7:3–4.
11. Moroni 7:47.
12. See Moroni 7:48.
13. Moroni 7:48.
14. See Moroni 7:45.
15. Mosiah 18:8.
16. Mosiah 18:9.
17. See Alma 24:19.
18. See 1 Corinthians 13:11.
19. See Doctrine and Covenants 109:22, 26.
20. 3 Nephi 12:14.
21. 2 Nephi 26:33.

Chapter 6: Treasure Your Family

1. The Resurrection will come to all because of Christ's victory over death. See Alma 11:41–45; 40; Doctrine and Covenants 76; Moses 7:62.
2. See Russell M. Nelson, "Salvation and Exaltation," *Ensign*, May 2008, 7–10.
3. Doctrine and Covenants 132:7; emphasis added.
4. Luke 18:22.
5. See John 11:35; Moses 7:28–29.
6. See Doctrine and Covenants 76:50–70.
7. See Mosiah 2:41; Alma 28:12.
8. See Doctrine and Covenants 132:7.
9. Doctrine and Covenants 49:16.
10. See Doctrine and Covenants 2:1–3; 138:48; Joseph Smith—History 1:38–39.
11. Doctrine and Covenants 49:16. See also Genesis 2:24; Matthew 19:5; Mark 10:7–9; Doctrine and Covenants 42:22; Moses 3:24; Abraham 5:18.
12. 1 Corinthians 11:11.
13. See Matthew 19:6.
14. See Doctrine and Covenants 132:19–20.
15. Moses 5:4; emphasis added.
16. See Doctrine and Covenants 109:8–9.
17. Psalm 127:3.
18. See Doctrine and Covenants 93:40.
19. George Pozgar, *Legal and Ethical Issues for Health Professionals* (Sudbury: Jones and Bartlett, 2010).
20. Gordon B. Hinckley, *Standing for Something: Ten Neglected Virtues That Will Heal Our Hearts and Homes* (New York: Random House), 2000, 45.
21. See Allan C. Carlson and Paul T. Mero, *The Family in America*, The Howard Center and the Sutherland Institute, 2005, 27–28. See also

Richard G. Wilkins, "The Society Role of the Family," World Policy Center.

22. "The Children I Never Had," *Ladies' Home Journal*, August 2005, 72.

Chapter 7: Respect the Spiritual Strength of Women

1. Neal A. Maxwell, "The Women of God," *Ensign*, May 1978.
2. Moses 4:26.
3. Elder L. Tom Perry passed away on May 30, 2015, followed by President Boyd K. Packer on July 3.
4. See Genesis 27:46; 28:1–4.
5. See Joseph Fielding Smith, *Answers to Gospel Questions*, comp. Joseph Fielding Smith Jr., 5 vols., 1957–66, 4:166.
6. Doctrine and Covenants 121:27–28.
7. Spencer W. Kimball, "The Role of Righteous Women," *Ensign*, November 1979.
8. "Relief Society—An Aid to the Priesthood," *Relief Society Magazine*, January 1959, 4, 5. See also Dallin H. Oaks, "The Keys and Authority of the Priesthood," *Ensign*, May 2014.
9. See Spencer J. Condie, *Russell M. Nelson: Father, Surgeon, Apostle* (Salt Lake City: Deseret Book, 2003), 146, 153–56. It is an ironic sidenote that in 1964, President Kimball set me apart as a stake president and blessed me that the mortality rates would decline in my pioneering efforts with operations on the aortic valve. Little did either of us then know that eight years later, I would be doing an operation on him that included replacement of his failed aortic valve.
10. Spencer W. Kimball, "Privileges and Responsibilities of Sisters," *Ensign*, November 1978.
11. See Doctrine and Covenants 25:7, 8, 10, 16.
12. Doctrine and Covenants 107:18.
13. Doctrine and Covenants 109:22.
14. See Doctrine and Covenants 131:2–4.
15. See Russell M. Nelson, "Lessons from Eve," *Ensign*, November 1987.
16. Gordon B. Hinckley, "The Women in Our Lives," *Ensign*, November 2004.

17. See Russell M. Nelson, "Children of the Covenant," *Ensign*, May 1995.

Chapter 8: Respect Priesthood Power

1. See full text of "Remarks and Dedicatory Prayer at Priesthood Restoration Site," September 19, 2015, http://newsroom.churchofJesusChrist.org/article/priesthood-restoration-site-dedication-transcript.
2. See *Teachings of the Prophet Joseph Smith*, sel. Joseph Fielding Smith (1976), 157–58, 166–67; see also Doctrine and Covenants 78:16.
3. Boyd K. Packer, "Priesthood Power in the Home," Worldwide Leadership Training Meeting, February 2012; see also James E. Faust, "Power of the Priesthood," *Ensign*, May 1997.
4. *Teachings of the Prophet Joseph Smith*, sel. Joseph Fielding Smith (1976), 157.
5. Joseph F. Smith, *Gospel Doctrine*, 5th ed. (1939), 139.
6. M. Russell Ballard, "Men and Women in the Work of the Lord," *New Era*, April 2014; see also *Daughters in My Kingdom: The History and Work of Relief Society* (2011), 138.
7. Doctrine and Covenants 112:30.
8. Doctrine and Covenants 107:18.
9. This experience preceded ministering.
10. Doctrine and Covenants 84:18.
11. See *Duties and Blessings of the Priesthood: Basic Manual for Priesthood Holders, Parts A and B* (2000); see also Alma 13:7–8; Doctrine and Covenants 84:17–20, 35–38; Moses 1:33, 35.
12. Doctrine and Covenants 121:36.
13. See Genesis 25:29–34.
14. See Genesis 12:3; 17:2–8; Galatians 3:29; 1 Nephi 15:14–18; Abraham 2:9–11.
15. Dallin H. Oaks, "The Keys and Authority of the Priesthood," *Ensign*, May 2014.
16. Doctrine and Covenants 132:47.
17. In 1962.
18. 2 Peter 1:4.
19. See 2 Peter 1:5–10.

20. See Doctrine and Covenants 4:6. Here, in a revelation to Joseph Smith, the Lord added *humility* to Peter's list.
21. Enos 1:2, 4.
22. See 2 Nephi 32:3.
23. See 2 Nephi 31:2–21.
24. Doctrine and Covenants 109:8.
25. See Doctrine and Covenants 84:19–20.
26. Doctrine and Covenants 4:7.
27. Doctrine and Covenants 84:33.
28. See Doctrine and Covenants 84:33–40.
29. Henry B. Eyring, "Faith and the Oath and Covenant of the Priesthood," *Ensign*, May 2008.

Chapter 9: Experience the Healing Power of Gratitude

1. Lisa Firestone, "The Healing Power of Gratitude," psychologytoday .com, November 19, 2015.
2. In Carolyn L. Todd, "The Healing Powers of Gratitude," Self.com, May 29, 2020.
3. David Brooks, "The Structure of Gratitude," nytimes.com, July 28, 2015.
4. Psalm 92:1.
5. Psalm 136:1.
6. Psalm 95:2.
7. Psalm 136:2.
8. 1 Thessalonians 5:18.
9. See 1 Nephi 18:10–16.
10. Joseph Smith, "Letter to Emma Smith, 4 April 1839," 1–2, joseph smithpapers.org. Spelling, punctuation, and capitalization are standardized.
11. Doctrine and Covenants 123:17; emphasis added.
12. Arthur C. Brooks, "Choose to Be Grateful. It Will Make You Happier," newyorktimes.com, November 21, 2015.
13. George Washington, "Thanksgiving Proclamation, 3 October 1789," *Founders Online,* National Archives, https://founders.archives.gov /documents/Washington/05-04-02-0091.

14. Genesis 12:3.
15. Luke 22:42.
16. Doctrine and Covenants 128:22.
17. Alma 37:37.

Chapter 10: Know That with God You Can Accomplish the Impossible

1. See 1 Samuel 17:49–50.
2. 1 Nephi 18:2.
3. See 1 Nephi 17–18.
4. See 1 Corinthians 1:27.
5. Alma 37:6.
6. Doctrine and Covenants 101:4–5.
7. 1 Corinthians 1:27.
8. Luke 1:37; emphasis added.
9. See Matthew 11:28–30; Alma 7:12–13; Ether 12:27.
10. Moroni 10:7.
11. Alma 32:27; emphasis added.
12. Matthew 17:20, emphasis added; see also Helaman 12:9, 13.
13. See Doctrine and Covenants 78:17–18.
14. Matthew 7:8.
15. See Mosiah 17:7–20.
16. See Ether 13:13–14; Moroni 1:1–3.
17. See Melvin L. Bashore, H. Dennis Tolley, and the BYU Pioneer Mortality Team, "Mortality on the Mormon Trail, 1847–1868," *BYU Studies*, vol. 53, no. 4, 2014, 115.
18. See Psalm 121:4.
19. Mormon 9:9.
20. See Mormon 9:10–11, 15.

Chapter 11: Honor Your Body

1. 1 Samuel 16:7.
2. See John 2:19–21.
3. 1 Corinthians 3:16, 17.
4. "The Family: A Proclamation to the World," ChurchofJesusChrist.org.

5. Job 38:7.
6. *Teachings of the Prophet Joseph Smith,* sel. Joseph Fielding Smith (1976), 181.
7. Alma 5:14.

Chapter 12: Listen to Latter-day Prophets

1. See Spencer J. Condie, *Russell M. Nelson: Father, Surgeon, Apostle* (Salt Lake City: Deseret Book, 2003), 165.
2. Harold B. Lee, letter to Ezra Taft Benson, in Sheri L. Dew, *Ezra Taft Benson: A Biography* (Salt Lake City: Deseret Book, 1987), 224.
3. Dew, *Ezra Taft Benson*, viii.
4. Gordon B. Hinckley, "Look to the Future," *Ensign*, November 1997.
5. Gordon B. Hinckley, "We Have a Work to Do," *Ensign*, May 1995.
6. Joseph Smith, "Church History," *Times and Seasons*, March 1, 1842, 707.
7. For an in-depth study of these visits, see "Seventy-six Accounts of Joseph Smith's Visionary Experiences," in John W. Welch, ed., *Opening the Heavens: Accounts of Divine Manifestations*, 1820–1844 (Provo, UT: Brigham Young University Studies, 2017), 302–9.
8. See Doctrine and Covenants 76:20–21; 137:1–6.
9. Doctrine and Covenants 137:1, 3.
10. See School of the Prophets Salt Lake City meeting minutes, October 3, 1883, 59, Church History Library, Salt Lake City.
11. Doctrine and Covenants 110:2–4.
12. See Joseph Smith "Journal, 1835–36," 24, josephsmithpapers.org.
13. Doctrine and Covenants 128:21.
14. *Teachings of Presidents of the Church: Joseph Smith* (2007), 419.
15. President George Q. Cannon was a counselor to Presidents Brigham Young, John Taylor, Wilford Woodruff, and Lorenzo Snow.
16. "Discourse by President George Q. Cannon," *Deseret Evening News*, February 10, 1883, 1.
17. See H. Donl Peterson, "Moroni—Joseph Smith's Tutor," *Ensign*, January 1992; Robert J. Woodford, "Book of Mormon Personalities Known by Joseph Smith," *Ensign*, August 1978.
18. Joseph Smith—History 1:34.

19. Joseph Smith—History 1:42.
20. Joseph Smith—History 1:54.
21. Joseph Smith—History 1:33.
22. John Taylor, in *Journal of Discourses,* 21:94.
23. See Doctrine and Covenants 110; 107:42–57; Joseph Smith discourse, January 5, 1841, in L. John Nuttall papers, L. Tom Perry Special Collections, Harold B. Lee Library, Brigham Young University, Provo, Utah; John Taylor, in *Journal of Discourses,* 17:374; George Q. Cannon, in *Journal of Discourses,* 13:47.
24. Doctrine and Covenants 38:32.
25. In addition to the sources listed in the previous notes, see, for example, Doctrine and Covenants 27:8–13; 128:20–21; John Taylor, in *Journal of Discourses,* 18:325–26; 21:65; 23:48–49.
26. See Doctrine and Covenants 27:12–13.
27. See Doctrine and Covenants 110.
28. John Taylor, in *Journal of Discourses,* 21:94.
29. Title Page of the Book of Mormon.
30. 1 Nephi 13:28.

Chapter 13: Immerse Yourself in the Word

1. See 2 Nephi 25:26.
2. Title Page of the Book of Mormon.
3. Isaiah 29:14.
4. In Isaiah's prophecy that the Lord's name one day should be called "Wonderful, Counsellor, The mighty God," etc. (Isaiah 9:6), the word *wonderful* is similar in meaning to wonder in Isaiah 29:14. Both come from the Hebrew *pele.*
5. From April to June 1828, Joseph translated 116 pages that Martin Harris later lost. For a season, Joseph's ability to translate was suspended (see Doctrine and Covenants 10:1–2). The process of translation was resumed on Tuesday, April 7, 1829.
6. See Doctrine and Covenants 6; 7; 8; 9; 10; 11; 12; 14; 15; 16; 17; 18.
7. See John W. Welch, "How long did it take Joseph Smith to translate the Book of Mormon?" *Ensign,* January 1988. It is estimated that the

original manuscript of the Book of Mormon numbered 607 pages, primarily written in Oliver Cowdery's hand.

8. Joseph Smith—History 1:71, note.
9. Emma Smith, in Edmund C. Briggs, "A Visit to Nauvoo in 1856," *Journal of History*, vol. 9, no. 4, October 1916, 454.
10. Emma Smith, in "Last Testimony of Sister Emma," *Saints' Herald*, October 1, 1879, 290.
11. See, for example, 2 Nephi 26.
12. 2 Nephi 29:8.
13. See Alma 12:15.
14. See 2 Nephi 9:41–46.
15. See 2 Nephi 3:6–21.
16. Joseph Smith, *Personal Writings of Joseph Smith*, ed. Dean C. Jessee, rev. ed. 2002, 449; spelling standardized.
17. See Ether 13:2, 8.
18. See 1 Nephi 2:20.
19. See Romans 5:11.
20. *Atonement*, 28; *atone*, 5; *atoning*, 3; *atoneth*, 3.
21. Moroni 10:4.
22. See Introduction to the Book of Mormon.
23. 3 Nephi 29, chapter heading.
24. See 3 Nephi 17:9–12.
25. Alma 13:27.

Chapter 14: Learn to Receive Personal Revelation

1. Alma 34:24, 26.
2. See 3 Nephi 28:1.
3. *Teachings of Presidents of the Church: Joseph Smith* (2007), 393–94.
4. See James 1:5.
5. *Teachings of Presidents of the Church: Joseph Smith* (2007), 132.
6. Doctrine and Covenants 121:33.
7. Moroni 10:5.
8. Doctrine and Covenants 42:61.
9. Neal A. Maxwell, "Meek and Lowly" (Brigham Young University devotional, October 21, 1986), speeches.byu.edu.

10. 2 Nephi 32:3.
11. See Isaiah 5:20; 2 Nephi 15:20.
12. See 2 Nephi 25:4; Alma 5:43.
13. Mark 9:7; Luke 9:35.
14. 3 Nephi 11:7.
15. Joseph Smith—History 1:17.
16. See Doctrine and Covenants 1:1.

Chapter 15: Make the Temple Your Spiritual Foundation

1. See "Sinking feeling: San Francisco's Millennium Tower is still leaning 3 in every year," theguardian.com, January 10, 2022; see also Katherine Clarke, "Penthouse Atop San Francisco's Millennium Tower Asks $14M," wsj.com, May 15, 2023.
2. See Doctrine and Covenants 109:22.
3. Doctrine and Covenants 38:30; see also 10:55.
4. 2 Timothy 3:1.
5. 2 Timothy 3:2–4.
6. 2 Corinthians 4:8–9.
7. See, for example, Exodus 28:29.
8. Moses 5:5–6.
9. Bible Dictionary, "Temple."
10. Numbers 9:15.
11. Exodus 38:21.
12. 1 Nephi 18:3.
13. 2 Nephi 5:16.
14. Doctrine and Covenants 88:119.
15. See Doctrine and Covenants 110:13–16.
16. Joseph Smith, in *Saints: The Story of the Church of Jesus Christ in the Latter Days*, vol. 1, *The Standard of Truth, 1815–1846* (2018), 454.
17. Bruce A. Van Orden, "Temple finished before exodus," *Deseret News*, December 9, 1995, deseret.com; see also Richard O. Cowan, "Endowments bless the living and dead," *Church News*, August 27, 1988, thechurchnews.com.
18. *Discourses of Brigham Young*, sel. John A. Widtsoe (1954), 403–4.

19. Harold B. Lee, "God's Kingdom—A Kingdom of Order," *Ensign*, January 1971.
20. *The Discourses of Wilford Woodruff*, sel. G. Homer Durham (1946), 153–54.
21. See 3 Nephi 29:8–9.
22. See Doctrine and Covenants 131:2, 4.
23. See Doctrine and Covenants 132:7.
24. John A. Widtsoe, "Symbolism in the Temples," in Archibald F. Bennett, ed., *Saviors on Mount Zion* (1950), 163.
25. See Mosiah 4:29.

Chapter 16: Embrace the Correct Name of the Church

1. See *History of the Church*, 2:62–63, 126.
2. Russell M. Nelson, in "The Name of the Church," official statement, August 16, 2018, ChurchofJesusChrist.org.
3. Doctrine and Covenants 115:4.
4. 3 Nephi 27:7–8.
5. See Doctrine and Covenants 19:18.
6. See Moroni 4:3; Doctrine and Covenants 20:37, 77.
7. Benjamin De Hoyos, "Called to Be Saints," *Ensign*, May 2011.
8. See Doctrine and Covenants 121:33.

Chapter 17: Let God Prevail in Our Lives

1. See Genesis 17:5; Nehemiah 9:7.
2. See Bible Dictionary, "Abraham, covenant of."
3. See Genesis 32:30; also spelled as *Penuel* in Genesis 32:31.
4. See Genesis 32:28.
5. See Genesis 35:11–12.
6. For further study, see Topical Guide, "Israel, Scattering of."
7. Isaiah 54:7.
8. See Isaiah 11:11–12; 2 Nephi 21:11–12; Mosiah 15:11.
9. See *Encyclopedia of Mormonism* (1992), "Covenant Israel, Latter-Day," 1:330–31.
10. See recollection of John Taylor in *Teachings of Presidents of the Church: Joseph Smith* (2007), 231.

11. Exodus 19:5; Psalm 135:4.
12. Malachi 3:17; Doctrine and Covenants 101:3.
13. Exodus 19:6; see also Deuteronomy 14:2; 26:18–19.
14. 3 Nephi 20:27.
15. Abraham 2:10; see also Romans 8:14–17; Galatians 3:26–29.
16. 2 Nephi 26:33.
17. John 10:27.
18. Doctrine and Covenants 33:3, 6; emphasis added.
19. Isaiah 18:2.
20. 3 Nephi 12:16.
21. See "Hope of Israel," *Hymns* (1985), no. 259.

Chapter 18: Overcome the World and Find Rest

1. Joseph Smith—Matthew 1:36.
2. Matthew 11:28–30; emphasis added.
3. John 16:33.
4. Doctrine and Covenants 64:2; emphasis added.
5. See Alma 7:11–13.
6. 2 Nephi 28:14.
7. See Alma 22:18. King Lamoni's father modeled this repentant behavior.
8. Mosiah 5:7.
9. Mosiah 3:19; emphasis added.
10. See 2 Nephi 31; 3 Nephi 27:16–20.
11. Mosiah 2:41.
12. Ezra Taft Benson, "Jesus Christ—Gifts and Expectations," *Ensign*, December 1988.
13. See Truman G. Madsen, *The Temple: Where Heaven Meets Earth* (Salt Lake City: Deseret Book, 2008), 11.

INDEX